Walks
in
Orkney

Clan Walk Guides

Walks
in
Orkney

Mary Welsh

Maps and illustrations by
Rosemary Harward

First published Westmorland Gazette, 1994
Revised Edition Published by Clan Books, 1999

ISBN 1 873597 11 8

Clan Book Sales Ltd
Clandon House
The Cross, Doune
Perthshire
FK16 6BE

Printed by
Cordfall Ltd, Glasgow

Foreword

The scale of Orkney lends itself to walking. Driving is a transitory pleasure; an hour will take you to any corner of the 'Mainland'; many islands will not even warm your engine before you run out of road! Walking, on the other hand, slows you down to an island pace and allows the sights, sounds and smells to be appreciated to their fullest. Whether this is an imaginary trip back through the centuries to walk through the Neolithic, Pictish or Norse landscapes, or a ramble to search for the plants and birds that make the islands unique, walking is a much more sensible way of enjoying our island heritage.

This book, which will be an asset to the islands, encourages you to explore them by following old tracks and less-used highways, as well as routes developed by the local authority. Most, but not all, the routes within the pages of this book are 'rights of way'. Over some, public passage is tolerated by the landowner; indeed walkers are tolerated almost anywhere as long as they show respect for common-sense privacy and the environment from which islanders must make their living.

This book does not represent the only opportunities for walking in Orkney. The local authority, in association with Scottish Natural Heritage, is committed to increasing the number and variety of routes where public access is catered for, whether in terms of providing stiles and waymakers at one extreme to car parks and leaflets at the other. The RSPB, likewise, has a progressive attitude to access on its reserves.

So, whether you relish the prospect of a whole day's walking, or are content with an hour-long stroll, put your best foot forward and enjoy our heritage.

Thomas W Eggeling
Director of Planning and Museums
November 1993

Acknowledgments

My grateful thanks go to Maureen Fleming, who walked every mile with me, constantly researching and checking; to Piers Blaxter of the Orkney Islands Council's Department of Planning and Museums, who gave me much help in planning the walks; to Eric Meek and his staff of the RSPB, who suggested routes that were pleasant to walk but at the same time created no disturbance to nesting birds; to P & O Scottish Ferries, for their interest and support; to Jean Cowling, who has once again carefully copy-edited the text; to my husband, Tom Welsh, for his ever-ready support; and, especially, to Rosemary Harward, for the illustrations and the cover picture, which so enhance the 42 walks.

Author's Note

A map reference is given in the information details at the beginning of each walk. Landranger maps can be used, but Pathfinders give more detail and were used by the author.

Good walking!

Map of Orkney

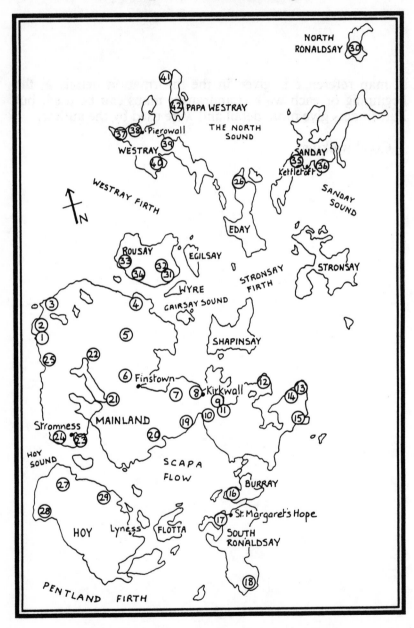

NORTH RONALDSAY ③⓪

④①

④② PAPA WESTRAY

THE NORTH SOUND

③⑦ ③⑧ Pierowall

WESTRAY ③⑨

④⓪

SANDAY ③⑤ ③⑥
Kettletoft

②⑥

SANDAY SOUND

WESTRAY FIRTH

N

EDAY

ROUSAY
③③ ③②
③④ ③①
WYRE

EGILSAY

STRONSAY

STRONSAY FIRTH

③ ④ CAIRSAY SOUND

② ①
⑤

②⑤ ②②

SHAPINSAY

⑥ Finstown

⑦ ⑧ Kirkwall ⑫ ⑬
② ① ⑨ ⑭
⑩ ⑪ ⑮
②① ⑲

MAINLAND

Stromness
②④ ②③ ②⓪

HOY SOUND

SCAPA FLOW

②⑦ BURRAY
②⑨ ⑯

②⑧ St. Margaret's Hope
Lyness ⑰
HOY FLOTTA SOUTH RONALDSAY

⑱

PENTLAND FIRTH

Contents

Contents (continued)

1. A Circular Walk over the RSPB Reserve at Marwick Head

Information	
Distance:	2½ miles
Time:	2 hours
Map:	Landranger 6, Pathfinder 28 Dounby, reference HY 229242 (parking)
Terrain:	Steady climb to the Head. Take great care along the cliff tops. Not to be attempted if winds too strong.
Status of access:	Right of way/Path over RSBP land

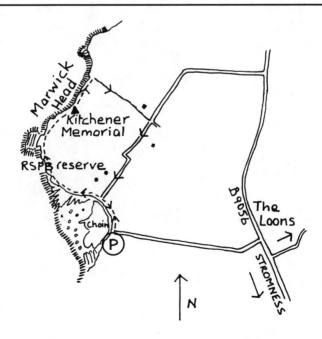

Marwick Head lies in the north-west corner of Mainland, about 11 miles north of Stromness. Leave the B9056 at Marwick, by the turn signposted for the reserve car park, which is situated just above the shore.

From the car park, walk north, with Mar Wick Bay to your left, along the track that skirts the shore. It is protected from the worst of the sea's force by a buttressed wall. Here grows a profusion of sea mayweed and sea campion. Sometimes, after

Marwick Head buttressed wall

a storm, boulders from the shore and the wall obliterate the path — so be warned. Follow the signpost for Marwick Head, pass through a kissing-gate and continue on the walled track.

Look back and to your left for a good view of the island of Hoy. Pass through the next kissing-gate and walk left to follow a track that soon becomes grassy, with shallow cliffs now immediately to your left. Constantly a great variety of birds fly overhead and out to sea. Look for gannets, great skuas, kittiwakes, fulmars, both the black-backed gulls, razorbills, guillemots, puffins and shags.

Dawdle on the steadily climbing path, which is bordered with a carpet of sea thrift, sea campion and orache. It brings you to the top of Marwick Head. A dramatic view of sheer cliffs, composed of old red sandstone, awaits you. Take care as you view.

Many ledges are occupied by rows of razorbills, most with their backs to the sea. On others stand long rows of guillemots, with glossy brownish-black plumage. Puffins sit alone or in small groups, preening, or disappearing into holes in the cliff face to feed their young. All other ledges seem taken up by innumerable fulmars, crooning to each other and their young. There is a constant coming and going as the adult birds seek food for their chicks. The food is sought out in the sea beyond the head, where the waters of the Atlantic and the North Sea mix and teem with fish. Occasionally a graceful arctic skua, with swift and powerful flight, victimises a guillemot until it throws up food. Similarly, a great skua chases a gull until it disgorges a half-digested fish. A pair of ravens fly grumbling overhead. The smell of the birds' droppings is very strong.

When you can drag yourself away from viewing this magnificent cliff face, continue to the foot of the Kitchener Memorial. It was erected to commemorate Lord Kitchener, Minister of War,

Arctic skua chasing guillemot

11

and the crew of *HMS Hampshire* who died when the boat was sunk by a mine on 5th June, 1916. Walk on and look back for another superb view of the headland, and then turn right through a metal kissing-gate.

The fenced track ahead is lined with summer flowers. Pass through a red kissing-gate and at the track end look for an old gun, salvaged from the wreck of the *Hampshire*. Then turn right to walk a lane, continuing where it ceases to be metalled past a modern house. Follow the track as it swings left to join another lane. Turn right and walk to the kissing-gate on the left. Beyond, walk beside the buttressed wall to rejoin your car.

As you drive away from the car park, head back to the B9056, and turn right and then left to reach the roadside hide of The Loons, a 180-acre marshland site owned by the RSPB (Royal Society for the Protection of Birds). There is as yet no access to the marshland itself. It is a basin mire enclosed by low sandstone hills.

In spring widgeon and pintail duck breed here and large numbers of green plover, snipe, dunlin, arctic tern and black-headed and common gull nest. In winter the marsh is flooded. Few marshes remain in Orkney. Many have been drained and used for agriculture.

2. A Linear Walk from Marwick Head to the Earl's Palace at Birsay

---

Information

Distance:	5 miles
Time:	2-3 hours
Map:	Landranger 6, Pathfinder 28 Dounby, reference HY 233252 (parking)
Terrain:	Easy walking all the way but take great care along the cliff edge.
Status of access:	Right of way

To reach the car park for the Kitchener Memorial, leave Stromness by the A965 and head north on the A967. Turn left at Twatt in the direction of Marwick, then right on to the B9056, and then take the second left at the signpost for Cumlaquoy (quoy meaning enclosure) and the Kitchener Memorial. Leave your car in the car park with the cannon (seen on Walk 1) from *HMS Hampshire*. From the small parking area you can see the memorial peeping over the cliff top.

Walk the fenced track, which climbs steadily to a kissing-gate from where there is a spectacular view left towards Hoy. Continue up the grassy way to another kissing-gate onto Marwick Head, where you are reminded that the cliffs are dangerous and you are asked to take care.

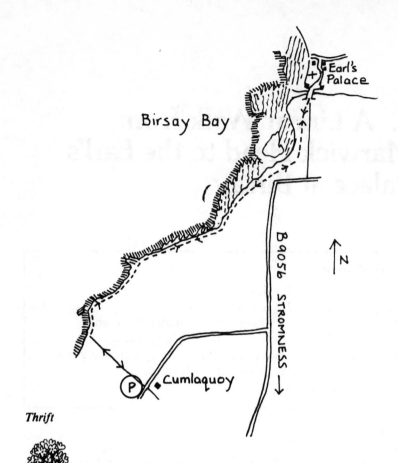

Birsay Bay

Earl's Palace

B9056 STROMNESS →

↑N

P • Cumlaquoy

Thrift

Beyond, bear right to walk the narrow path, which is bordered with thrift, kidney vetch, eyebright, wild thyme, crowberry, dark purple orchis, yarrow and buttercups. The path lies close to the edge of the glorious rose pink cliffs. The layers of sandstone look almost hewn ready for use. Look for kittiwakes in their hundreds, flying into their nesting sites, and a couple of great skuas gliding along the cliff edge, causing the fulmars to scold from their ledges. Guillemots pause and preen on other shelves apart from the

crowd. On a sunny face of a cliff each ledge is occupied by several puffins.

Stroll on along the steadily descending path towards Birsay Bay. Look for seals snoozing on rocks and peering curiously from the water. Families of eider swim together and others sunbathe on plates of sandstone. A crowd of shags sit together on another projecting rock. Redshanks give their haunting calls as they hurry over the shore.

Ahead, with grassy slopes and steep cliffs, stands the Brough of Birsay, encircled with a blue sea. To the right catch a glimpse of Rousay and the distant cliffs of Westray. When you reach a grassy cart-track, colourful with pink clover, follow it for a few yards and then, where it swings right, pass through the fence. Walk diagonally right over the greensward to join a grassy track, continuing ahead and edging an area of exposed sand. Stride on to pass through a metal gate and onto a track to the road. Turn left and cross the swiftly-flowing Burn of Boardhouse on an attractive stone bridge to walk into the village of Birsay. The pleasing odour of peat smoke hangs over the dwellings.

Dominating the cottages are the magnificent ruins of the Earl's Palace. The notorious Robert Stewart, Earl of Orkney, founded the palace in 1574. It was completed by his even more

15

unpleasant son, Earl Patrick, and consisted of four ranges round an open courtyard, with projecting towers at three of the four corners. The walls have many gun loops and there is a well in the courtyard. Colourful plaques provided by Historic Scotland, in whose care the palace is, show a wealthy man's home and the courtyard as a place of much activity.

Visit the church of St Magnus, which was built in 1760. Two earlier churches may have stood on the site. Look for the old gravestones lying flat. Several record burials in the middle of the 18th century.

Return by the same route to rejoin your car.

3. A Circular Walk via the Brough of Birsay, Fishermen's Hut and Skipi Geo

Information

Distance:	3½ miles
Time:	2 hours
Map:	Landranger 6, Pathfinder 28 Dounby, reference HY 248277 (parking)
Terrain:	Easy walking but stout shoes are advisable for crossing the causeway.
Status of access:	Right of way

Head north from Stromness by the A965 and the A967 and continue in the direction of Northside, in the north-west of Mainland. Turn left onto the A966, passing the Earl's Palace (Walk 2) on your left, and follow the lane above the shore to the car park at the Point of Buckquoy.

Drop down the steps to the sand and rock flags of Brough Sound and cross the man-made causeway to the historic island Brough of Birsay. A variety of seaweeds can be seen as you walk the short concrete strand. The sea has deeply eroded the cliffs here. Notice the attempt being made to control this erosion — the method used repeats the natural layering of the sandstone. Climb a ramp to reach the island.

Before the Norse settlers came here to Orkney from Scandinavia, this area was already occupied by Picts and there are traces of Pictish settlements on both sides of the sound. On the Brough of Birsay you will see the evidence of an early Celtic Christian settlement and the much more obvious remains of Norse houses and a 12th-century church.

The body of St Magnus was buried at Birsay after his murder on Egilsay in 1117 and his body lay either in the church in the village or on the Brough. It was taken to Kirkwall a few years later. The Brough remained a place of pilgrimage until a few centuries ago.

Puffins

Pass through the hand gate behind the small shop and museum and walk beside the fence to a kissing-gate (where you are asked to keep all dogs on a lead) and onto the short greensward. The path leads up the slope, where sheep graze, to the foot of the lighthouse (built in 1925). From here there is a spectacular

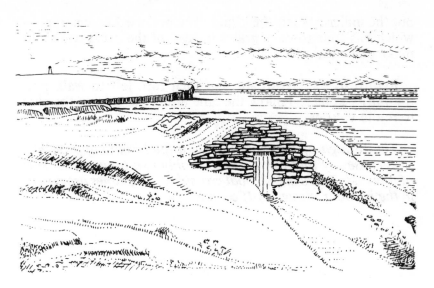

Fishermen's hut

view. Take care as you approach the edge of the high sheer cliffs, which are home to fulmars and puffins.

Return across the causeway, with a good view of the cliffs of Westray. Follow the signpost for the Skipi Geo and walk a wide grassy path, which is bordered with colourful flowers. The geo, or creek, is a sheltered bay and with its gently-sloping beach it forms a natural harbour. It has been used by fishermen since Viking times. Look for the flagged way down to the shore and the pleasingly restored turf-roofed hut, also used by fishermen in the past. Close by the hut are boat-shaped depressions, nousts, where boats were stored.

Head on along the grassy path as it continues by the cliff edge to come to a bone from a whale that has been stuck on the cliff top and looks, from the distance, like a petrified owl. Follow the track as it swings inland towards the dwellings of Northside. Here many of the buildings have flagged roofs. Cross the narrow road and walk ahead along a narrow road where a farmer cuts his hay. At the crossroads, continue ahead to see Boardhouse Mill, with its three wheels, sited on the burn that flows out of the Loch of Boardhouse. It was in use until 1993 but the miller has left the island. The mill used bere barley — which has four rows of grains instead of the usual two — to make bere meal (see Walk 4).

Return to the crossroads and then turn left to walk past the Earl's Palace. Follow the lane along the side of the cliff to rejoin your car.

The Brough of Birsay stands on a tidal island approached by a causeway that can be crossed only two hours either side of low tide. There are no boat crossings. Tide times are posted in the harbour master's office in Kirkwall.

4. A Circular Walk from the Sands of Evie via the Broch of Gurness

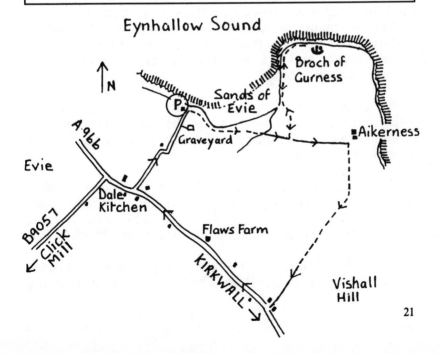

From Finstown, drive north on the A966 to the village of Evie, which lies to the north-east of Mainland. Leave the village by taking a turning off the A966 opposite the Dale Kitchen. Drive the narrow road to the end of the tarmac and leave your car in the tiny car park at Evie Sands. There are good toilets, a picnic table, seats and an information room set up in an old fishing hut.

Return to the tarmac road and walk along the continuing rough track. Enjoy the perfect arc of sand where seals peep out of the water and eiders marshall their young. The track is lined with a glorious array of flowers. Across Eynhallow Sound you can see Westness Farm and House on the Island of Rousay and most of the Westness Walk (Walk 34). To the right is a field of barley with deep-blue bugloss flowering in the margins.

Bugloss

Follow the arrow for the Broch of Gurness and continue along the flower-bordered track. To the left you can see the aerogenerators on Burgar Hill and the cliffs of western Rousay. Look for heartsease growing on the sandy edges of the track and a lovely mauve yarrow. Here meadow pipits flit about the pastures and a family of pied wagtails sit on fence posts. Look for sea rocket and sea mayweed flowering on the sands. Beyond, men fish for saithe.

Pass through the official car park to enter the enclosure in which lies the broch. It stands on the tip of the Aikerness promontory and is in the care of Historic Scotland. There is a small entrance fee.

The broch was discovered in 1929 by an Orkney scholar, Robert Rendall. He was sketching, sitting on a mound above the shore, when he lost the leg of his stool in a hole and dug down to reveal a staircase on the west side of the broch tower.

The thick walled tower, or broch, was probably built in the first century BC for a chieftain. The thickness of the walls and the number of doorways to be passed through indicates the importance of the chief. Around the broch were three lines of defensive ramparts and ditches. The entrance was through a long passage ·on the eastern side and visitors would have approached by sea. Wander round the site and try to imagine what it must have been like.

Later, outside the tower and within the inner ditch, was built a village where thirty families might have lived. By this time the broch was no longer of defensive importance but may have been lived in as another dwelling.

The village as you look at it is now a ruin. The roofs and the tops of the walls are all gone. Two thousand years ago this would have been a busy farming settlement with people always wary of competitive and sometimes aggressive neighbours.

Inside the broch is a well with steps down. Pictish artefacts have been found and also the grave of a wealthy ninth century Norse woman.

Return along the track beside the bay, where kittiwakes, fulmars and shags fly up the sound. An arctic skua sits on the edge of the water watching a crowd of noisy arctic terns hunting sand eels among seaweed on a rocky projection. One flies up with an eel dangling from its mouth. Suddenly the skua flies the tern down until the victim disgorges the eel. Then the furious tern mobs the unworried skua.

At the T-junction, turn left and walk the reinforced track until just before Aikerness Farm. Turn right and head along the continuing track below Vishall Hill. Cross two cattle grids. Beyond the second, large clumps of heather flourish and along the side of the track a white vetch grows. At the end of the track, turn right onto the A966.

Carry on by Flaws Farm, which has a large black cannon in its yard, pass Evie hostel and into the village of Evie. Stride on past the church and turn right opposite the Dale Kitchen to take the lane towards the car park. A small track on the right leads to a graveyard. Low growing trees of sycamore, willow and wych elm shadow some of the graves.

23

Walk on to rejoin your car.

Before you leave the area, you might wish to visit Orkney's only click mill. Turn right onto the A966 at Dale Kitchen and then left onto the B9057. The mill is well signposted and there is a lay-by for parking. Follow the grassy track from the lay-by to a kissing-gate. Beyond, head across the pasture to pass through another.

This little 19th-century corn mill used a horizontal water-wheel to drive the millstones, which were enclosed in a wooden casing. The bere barley was tipped into a hopper and then flowed into a hole in the centre of the upper stone. A wooden tongue kept the grain moving, and as it struck a stone projection on the top of the upper stone it made a distinctive 'click, click'. This mill would have served three or four households.

Click mill

5. A Linear Walk to the RSPB Hide at Lower Cottascarth

Information

Distance:	1 mile
Time:	As much time as you can spare
Map:	Landranger 6, Pathfinder 31 Finstown, reference HY 368195 (parking)
Terrain:	Easy walking for most of the way. The track becomes wet towards the end, and the rough pasture in front of the hide can be very wet. Boots required.
Status of access:	Path over RSPB land

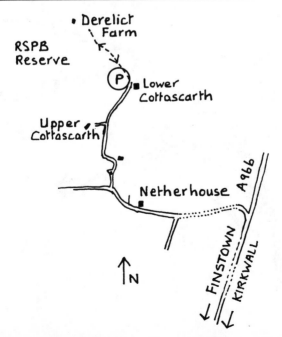

Head north from Finstown on the A966 and after some three miles turn left towards Netherhouse, and then take a right turn, signposted Cottascarth. At the end of the metalled track, just beyond the farmhouse, is a large P for parking. Drive on ten yards or so to park by the wall on the left.

An information panel at the start of the walk tells you the vegetation of Cottascarth has been called 'treeless woodland'; the natural vegetation of the area was once scrub woodland, which has largely disappeared, leaving only woodland floor plants, such as great woodrush. Cottascarth is the southern portion of the Birsay Moors RSPB reserve. There is access at all times and you are asked not to cause disturbance to nesting birds.

Walk ahead to take the arrowed second gate on the left. Stride the gradually climbing, fenced track, leaving all gates as you find them. Away to the right stand several short, twisted larch and clumps of gorse. Green plover, oyster-catchers and hoodie crows abound.

Keep to the left of the wire fence (arrowed) and turn right at the next arrow across rough wet pasture to the hide, which lies beyond a derelict farm and its surprisingly large sycamore.

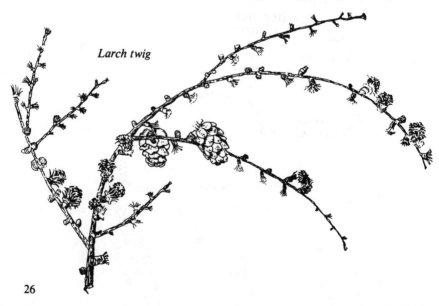

Larch twig

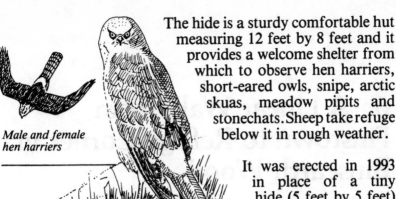

Male and female hen harriers

The hide is a sturdy comfortable hut measuring 12 feet by 8 feet and it provides a welcome shelter from which to observe hen harriers, short-eared owls, snipe, arctic skuas, meadow pipits and stonechats. Sheep take refuge below it in rough weather.

It was erected in 1993 in place of a tiny hide (5 feet by 5 feet) erected more than twenty years earlier by Eddie Balfour. Balfour's hide has been re-erected in the Rendall Hills by a keen bird watcher.

Spend as much time as you can spare here and then return by the same route to rejoin your car.

6. A Linear Walk from Finstown to Refuge Corner via Binscarth Wood

Information	
Distance:	3½ miles
Time:	2 hours
Map:	Landranger 6, Pathfinder 31 Finstown, reference HY 356141 (parking)
Terrain:	Easy walking all the way. Can be very muddy through Binscarth Wood.
Status of access:	Right of way

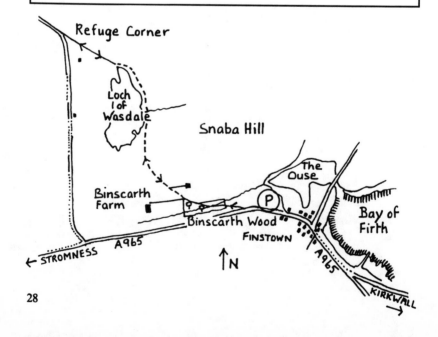

Leave your car in a lay-by at the western edge of Finstown. If you are travelling from Stromness, the lay-by lies on your left just before you enter the village. If travelling from Kirkwall you drive through the village, past the Pomona Hotel, and the lay-by lies on the right side of the road. Below lies the Ouse and beside it the old mill, which once ground bere.

Walk west for a few yards from the lay-by along the A965 and pass through the kissing-gate, signposted public footpath to Refuge Corner via Binscarth Wood. Bear left along a grassy terrace towards the wood. Pass through the kissing-gate and stroll down a track, passing below deciduous trees. A wren marshals its brood with much scolding, close by.

This is one of the few areas of woodland in Orkney. The seven-and-a-half acres were planted in the last century and provide nesting sites and sanctuary for birds in an island with virtually no hedges and few trees. By the next kissing-gate is an information panel on the wood.

Beyond the gate, walk the continuing path below beech, cherry, rowan, alder and sycamore. To your left hurries the Ouse. In July the woodland is carpeted with the pretty pink purslane, which replaces the bluebells of springtime. After a hundred yards, turn right up some stone steps to a stepped stile in the wall and rejoin the track. Turn left and walk uphill through great bushes of salmon berry, some of them laden with berries. Continue past a small larch plantation and then through another kissing-gate onto a stony track. To the right stands Binscarth, a fine sturdy house. Head on along the wide walled way, as directed by the waymark, with wind-stunted trees on both sides.

Where the path swings right, walk ahead along a signposted grassy track. Look left through the trees to see the picturesque Binscarth Farm. The way now passes out into more open countryside, with the skirts of Snaba Hill covered with gorse. To the left, in the open pastures, dozens of young rooks feed — these are some of the birds that will use Binscarth Wood for roosting.

Binscarth Farm

Follow the delightful path through a colourful array of wild flowers to a metal gate. Beyond lies the Loch of Wasdale, where several anglers fish for trout. Dawdle *Marsh* along the loch side, on whose banks grow meadow *orchid* sweet, pink campion, foxgloves, scabious, flags, water avens, wild parsley and a myriad of wild grasses. Watch for the black-headed gulls, which nest in the marsh beyond, hovering as they pick off dozens of small insects feeding on the umbels of hogweed. Several arctic terns fly from a small island on the loch and dive low over the still water.

Continue along the track beyond the loch. The marshland now on either side is ablaze with ragged robin. Bog cotton grows in profusion and there is a huge clump of water avens. Look for the broad-leaved marsh orchids, with deep purple flowers, growing in the damp grassy verges. Overhead fly several angry black-headed gulls determined to deter intruders who come too close to their nest site. And then Refuge Corner, named after a nearby house, is reached.

From here you could return by road, by turning left twice, but it is much more pleasant to return by the footpath and enjoy a different perspective for much of the way.

7. A Circular Walk to Wideford Cairn on Wideford Hill

Information	
Distance:	1 mile
Time:	1 hour
Map:	Landranger 6, Pathfinder 32 Kirkwall, reference HY 411114 (parking)
Terrain:	Walking boots advisable
Status of access:	Right of way

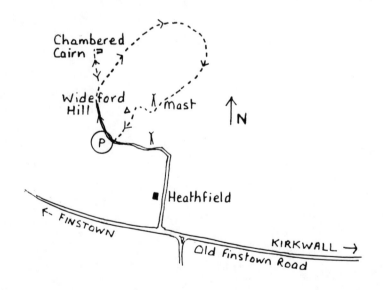

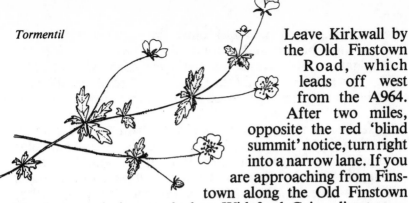

Tormentil

Leave Kirkwall by the Old Finstown Road, which leads off west from the A964. After two miles, opposite the red 'blind summit' notice, turn right into a narrow lane. If you are approaching from Finstown along the Old Finstown Road, a road sign marked to Wideford Cairn directs you left up the lane. Drive with care as the track is used by cattle and can be very muddy. The car park lies halfway up the hill on your left.

Take the signposted pitched footpath, which has regular finger posts to direct you on your way. The path, with superb views of Mull Head, Copinsay, Scapa Pier, Hoy, Finstown, Shapinsay, Rousay and the Bay of Firth, passes through heather and crowberry moorland, spangled with tormentil. Gulls hang in the thermals over the summit of the hill and meadow pipits flit over the low shrubs. About the path grow lousewort and hard fern.

Wideford Cairn

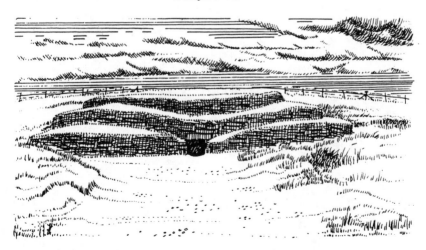

33

At the ditch, turn right and follow the signposted path left. Pass through the gate and continue along the clear track to the kissing-gate, which gives access to the enclosed Wideford Hill cairn. This is a communal tomb dating back to about 3000 BC placed on an artificially-levelled platform dug into the hillside.

Take the torch housed in a box and climb the mound to a trap door, from which a metal ladder descends to a rectangular stone chamber, large enough to stand up in, which has three cells leading from it. Heavy lintels are positioned over the cells and the passage. Ponder on the achievement of the people who, so long ago, created this impressive structure without the equipment we have today.

When you leave, do not forget to close the trap door and return the torch. Walk back along the narrow path to the gate and beyond turn left to walk a steadily climbing turfed way. From the top of a heather plant a stonechat scolds.

At an indistinct junction of tracks, strike right up the hill over the heather towards the radio transmitting station to join a track. Continue climbing to pass the trig point on your right beyond a wired enclosure. From here enjoy the magnificent view of the wide bay below. Follow one of the tracks left if you wish for a bird's eye view of Kirkwall and its harbour. If you have left the main track, return and follow it to rejoin your car.

8. A Walk through Kirkwall

Information

Distance:	1 mile
Time:	2 hours
Map:	Use map in Kirkwall Heritage Guide, obtained from Tourist Board. Landranger 6, Pathfinder 32 Kirkwall, reference HY 451108 (parking)
Parking:	Use St Magnus Lane Pay and Display car park off Junction Street
Status of access:	Right of way (roads)

Leave the car park and turn right and right again to walk St Magnus Lane. Cross Broad Street and enter the dramatic medieval St Magnus Cathedral (A), built of sandstone. The building was started in 1137 by Earl Rognvald Kolsson in memory of his murdered uncle Magnus Erlendsson. The bones of St Rognvald and St Magnus are deposited in the two piers on either side of the choir. Look for crosses etched on stones, high above your head in both piers. The remains have been removed and examined during this century and then returned. Wander through the aisles and read the solemn words on the huge gravestones.

Earl Rognvald

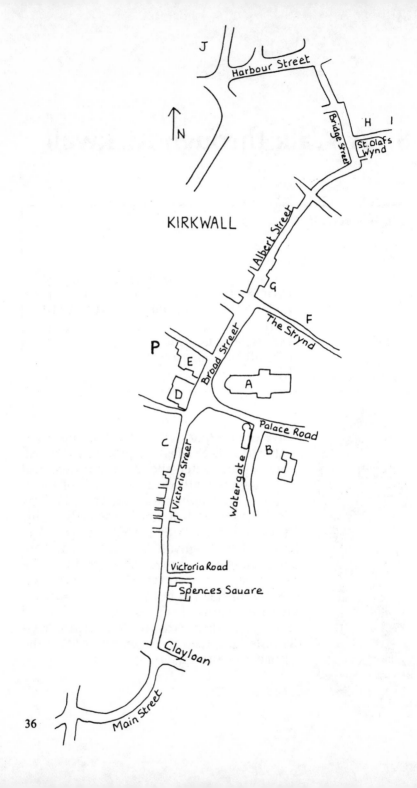

KIRKWALL

J

Harbour Street

Bridge Street

H I

St.Olafs Wynd

N

Albert Street

G

The Strynd

F

P

Broad Street

E

A

D

Palace Road

C

Victoria Street

Watergate

B

Victoria Road

Spences Sauare

Clayloan

Main Street

St Magnus Cathedral

On leaving the cathedral, walk left and turn up Palace Road to pass first the Bishop's Palace (B) and then the Earl's Palace. Enter the latter and walk beneath a row of sycamores to obtain a ticket to view the striking ruin, a fine example of French Renaissance architecture. Cross the road, Watergate,

37

to visit the ruin of the Bishop's Palace, built in the 12th century. Here Bishop William the Old could live close to his magnificent cathedral.

Return along Palace Road, bearing left to dawdle along the narrow paved Victoria Street (C). Look for the even narrower lanes leading off, providing access to houses built behind. Continue on to view Spences Square, with its 17th-century houses, which have Caithness slate roofs and deeply-recessed windows. Look for the decorative stones (skew-putts) on the gable ends that front onto the street. Cross Clay Loan and stroll along Main Street to its end between more old houses. This is the south-western boundary of Kirkwall's conservation area.

Walk back along Main and Victoria Street to Broad Street. On your left is Tankerness House (D). For three centuries it was the town dwelling of the Baikies family of Tankerness. Today it is a museum of Orkney life and well worth a visit. The dwelling has been restored to much of its former glory and provides a fine backcloth for the many exhibits. Walk in its extensive and pleasing garden, which is open to all.

Head on along Broad Street to pass the striking Town Hall (E), an example of Scottish baronial architecture. Cross the road and walk by the Tourist Board office. Turn right to climb the Strynd (F), a narrow passage with a picturesque group of buildings on the north side. The Strynd is named after a small stream that ran through it.

Return to Broad Street and turn right to continue along Albert Street, another fine narrow way. Here stands a sturdy sycamore tree (G). Apparently when the street was widened in 1870, the owner of the garden in which the tree stood insisted it be left untouched.

Follow the lane as it swings left and then turn right into St Olaf's Wynd to see a sandstone arched doorway (H) on your left. It has been rebuilt but is believed to date from 1550 when St Olaf's Kirk stood on the site.

Walk on along the Wynd and continue ahead along the unmade track behind the cottages on your right. Look for the two large sliding doors on your left. Pass through these and on through a storage area into a courtyard. Here stands a magnificent 18th-century folly (I), a garden house with a conical roof, which is ornately topped with volcanic rock. The rock is said to have come from the ballast of the *Revenge,* ship of the pirate John Gow.

Return to Bridge Street and continue to Harbour Street and turn left. Pass the Ayre Hotel and over the roundabout to walk the causeway road that runs between the Peerie (small) Sea (J) on the left and Kirkwall Bay on the right. The causeway has been built on an ayre, a spit of boulders, thrown up by the sea, isolating an area of 'dead' water (Peerie Sea) behind it. The hotel passed earlier is named after the natural phenomenon.

Return to the roundabout and turn right into Junction Road to rejoin your car.

9. A Circular Walk from Kirkwall via Seatter to Berstane Road Bridlepath

Information

Distance:	4 miles
Time:	1½-2 hours
Map:	Landranger 6, Pathfinder 32 Kirkwall, reference HY 448113 (parking)
Terrain:	Easy walking. The bridlepath is initially muddy.
Status of access:	Right of way

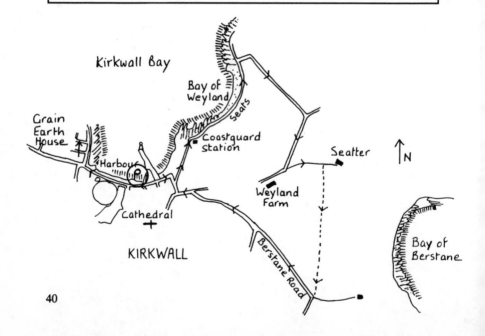

Mergansers

Park near to the harbour and walk east along the busy waterfront. Follow Shore Street round right to St Catherine's Place, and then turn left into Cromwell Road. Stride along the road, enjoying a good view of Kirkwall Bay. Continue past the coastguard station and out into a more rural area. Cross the road and stroll along a wide grassy area with seats overlooking the Bay of Weyland. Here curlews, red shanks and gulls probe for prey and eiders snooze on the water. A pair of mergansers dive excitedly for sand-eels near to the shore.

Follow the road as it swings right and inland. Its borders are lined with flowers; fuchsia, sycamore, elder, whitebeam and willow grow. At the T-junction bear right. Away to the right is an expansive view of the Wide Firth and to the left a field of barley trembles in a gentle breeze.

As you near Weyland Farm, with its tall silo, turn sharp left to walk a reinforced track that leads to Seatter Farm. Just before the dwelling, take the track on the right, signposted Berstane Road bridlepath. Pass through the red kissing-gate and stride along the rather muddy way. To the left is a wind-bent hawthorn hedge. Beyond the next kissing-gate, the grass has been cut and the wide way is a joy to walk. The hawthorn hedge is now to your right. To the left lies the pleasing Bay of Berstane in Inganess Bay. The Head of Work, the Head of Holland and Yinstay Head stretch out into the silvery sea like the fingers of a hand.

Stroll on, where pink purslane grows beneath willow, to the signposted exit to Berstane Road. Turn right and continue along the road. Look for a sighting of the cathedral and of

41

Wideford Hill. Follow the road as it swings right, now with the harbour coming into sight. Turn left into East Road and then right into St Catherine's Place. Cross the end of Cromwell Road, where you walked earlier, and then head on left along Shore Street to rejoin your car.

You might like to combine a visit to the earth house at Grain with the Seatter to Berstane walk. If so, walk west along Harbour Street. Continue past the Ayre Hotel and over the roundabout. Cross the causeway road, built on an ayre, and turn right as directed by the signpost. Call into Ortak, the silvercraft shop, to obtain the key and a large torch.

Turn left into Scots Road and follow the signpost for the earth house. Walk through the industrial estate for a quarter of a mile to where it lies on your right beneath a grassy mound. An information panel tells you that it was discovered in 1827. It is a well-preserved structure of a type that is found only in Orkney and Shetland. Descend stone steps and crouch as you

Grain stores

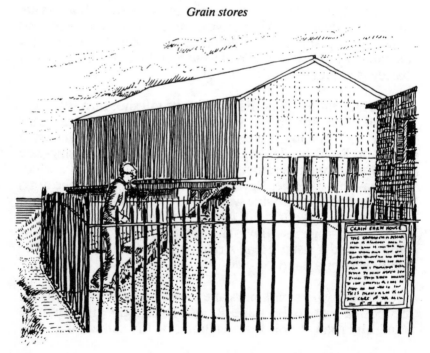

move along a passage leading to a chamber 12 feet long, 6 feet wide and 5 feet 6 inches high. The roof of the chamber, which is about 7 feet below the surface, is supported by four free-standing stone pillars. Earth houses like this may have been built about the second century AD. Their function is unknown. They may have served as a dwelling, a store, a workshop, or even as a hiding place.

It is an eerie and exciting place to visit, except for the claustrophobic. If it was a store, how appropriate to find it among modern-day storage buildings and workshops.

(The earth house is closed on Saturdays and Sundays and on weekdays the key must be obtained before 4.30 p.m.)

This walk is partly urban and partly rural with pleasing views for much of the way.

10. A Circular Walk via Scapa Pier

Information	
Distance:	3½ miles
Time:	1½ hours
Map:	Landranger 6, Pathfinder 34 Scapa Bay, reference HY 457088 (parking)
Terrain:	Easy walking but the bridleway, often used by horses, can be very muddy after rain.
Status of access:	Right of way

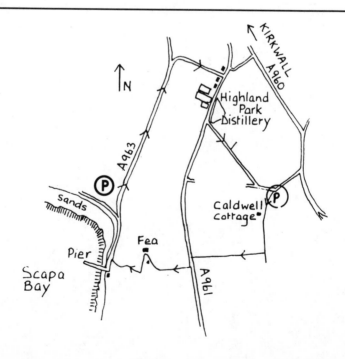

Leave Kirkwall by the A960, and ascend the hill out of the town. Follow the road as it bends right and turn right into a narrow unmarked lane. The start of the bridleway is 400 yards along. Park near a disused quarry.

Short-eared owl

Pass through a kissing-gate and stride the pleasing way in the direction of Caldwell Cottage. Look for a short-eared owl sitting on a fence post. It seems to watch the walker's approach and then takes off and moves a few posts along. It does this time and again. Finally it flies low over the pasture, and several green plovers rise from feeding and harry it until it moves out of sight. Oystercatchers and hoodie crows, also using the fence posts, remain unconcerned by the drama.

Continue along the track, which is lined with common mallow, tormentil, bedstraw, pink campion, pink clover and vetch. Yellow flags, wild watercress and milkmaids brighten the wet areas on either side. Gorse in bloom adds its brilliance to the colourful way. Curlews call from the pastures and fly overhead.

Follow the track as it swings right and is lined for a short way with low-growing whitebeam trees. Continue to the kissing-gate and on to the road, where you turn left. After 20 yards, turn right and walk a cart-track, where large-headed buttercups and ragwort grow, towards Fea. From here you can see Scapa Bay and the brightly-coloured large boats, which bring in gas, oil and petrol to its pier.

Carry on through the farm, with buildings to the right and a bungalow to your left, to drop down the continuing track. The route is very muddy but it is possible to pick your way and remain reasonably dry-shod. The track ends at the shore road. Out in the bay huge buoys of car tyres provide mooring for deep-water tankers and booms for the smaller vessels that take off their load of oil.

Pause to enjoy redshanks feeding on the shoreline. Look for a little group of female mergansers snoozing on the still water and a gathering of gossiping eiders. Head right along the road, where the cliffs on the right are a colourful mosaic of flowers.

Stride on along the road (A963) as it swings inland and continue for three-quarters of a mile to the T-junction. Turn right and climb the steep hill to bear right again at the top. Ahead is the Highland Park distillery, with its pagoda-like chimneys. Below these, peat fires dry the malt. Pass between the buildings, from where emanates a strong pleasing aroma. Cross the road and take the track that goes off left beyond the last building of the distillery to walk a walled track. Where the track swings left, walk straight ahead along the grassy way to pass a large number of greater knapweed. On reaching the tarmacked road, walk left to regain your car

Highland Park distillery

11. A Circular Walk from Wideford via Inganess

Information	
Distance:	3½ miles
Time:	2 hours
Map:	Landranger 6, Pathfinder 34 Scapa Bay, reference HY 457088 (parking)
Terrain:	Parts of the route are difficult to walk because lush vegetation obscures the indistinct paths. Walking boots essential.
Status of access:	Right of way

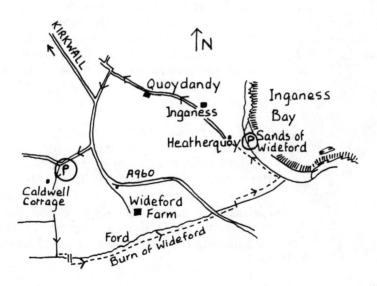

Park as you did for Walk 10 and again stride the access track to Caldwell Cottage. Pass through the kissing-gate and walk the wide grassy track, which is bordered with holly, gorse and scrubby hawthorn. In the pastures, starlings, herring gulls, hoodies, pigeons, oyster-catchers, black-backed gulls and curlews feed.

Where the good track swings right, press ahead along a much narrower fenced way, which is covered with dense vegetation. Cross the duckboarding at the end of the track and look for the narrow path continuing in the same direction. This passes through yellow flags, meadow sweet and rushes, and leads to the side of the Burn of Wideford.

Walk downstream for a few yards to a plank footbridge, almost hidden by vegetation, to cross to the opposite bank. Bear left past a waymarked post, almost obscured by a mass of summer flowers including the pretty marsh woundwort. Look here for a short-eared owl that sweeps low over the vegetation, probably hunting for an Orkney vole. Look too for tunnels under the rough grass made by this tiny mammal.

Yellow flags

This is a glorious part of the walk where banks of ragged robin, water dropwort, horse tail and marsh stitchwort flourish. The way now comes close beside the fence on your right and after crossing two tiny ditches you climb a rickety stile. Ahead is a pleasing view of the lovely Wideford valley, with a small glimpse of the sea beyond.

Continue beside the little burn to the next stile, waymarked, just above a ford. Stroll on and follow the path as it climbs above the meadow sweet and the flags. Straddle the next waymarked stile and walk below Wideford Farm, with its long roofed barn. It was here, in 1934, that a Captain Fresson flew, establishing the first internal airmail service in Britain.

Field scabious, hay rattle and eyebright, growing about the way, attract several meadow brown butterflies. You pass through plantings of willow, alder and rowan. Keep well up the slope, passing through scrub willow, to reach the next stile. Beyond, continue on to battle through some thick willow scrub and, on reaching the fence, climb up beside it to another waymarked stile.

Once over, stride on to a large clump of willows about the stream. Here the arrows are heavily encrusted with lichen. They direct you right, beside a fence on your left, to a gate to a track. Follow the track to the road, which you cross.

Climb the waymarked stile, opposite the cart-track, with the burn still to your left. Walk on towards the red painted footbridge. Here the cows have trodden a way for you through the flags, meadow sweet, pink campion and buttercups. Cross the bridge and continue downstream climbing a series of stiles over newly erected fences where the banks of the little burn are a brilliant blue with forget-me-nots. Small trout swim seawards.

Climb the next stile and press on, with a lagoon to the left. Here a wisp of snipe rise and circle the pool and then return to the muddy margins to probe for worms. A greenshank struts across the ooze. Head on through the common reed to the edge of another tributary stream. Walk left to the footbridge and then carry on over the few yards to the stile and onto a tarmacked track running above the Sand of Wideford. Look right to see a charming two-arched drystone bridge over a small burn where fish swim. Just off-shore lies a rusting wreck. It once supplied fresh water to ships during the Second World War. On its way to the scrapyard it ran aground in the bay and has been left to rust away.

From the stile turn left, north-west, to walk the grassy way. Enjoy the lovely arcing bay, its shallow cliffs covered with thrifts and grass almost to the water's edge. Climb the reinforced track by the windmill generating electricity. Pass the cottage of Heatherquoy and then Inganess Farm. Carry on by Quoydandy Farm. Then Kirkwall comes into view and the cathedral.

Inganess Bay

Take the next left turn and walk to the A960, where you turn left. After 250 yards, turn right to walk the narrow road to rejoin your car.

12. A Circular Walk round Rerwick Head, Tankerness

Information	
Distance:	¾ mile
Time:	1 hour
Map:	Landranger 6, Pathfinder 32 Kirkwall, reference HY 539116 (parking)
Parking:	Easy walking if you remain on the track. Boots advisable for scrambling on the rocks.
Status of access:	Path by tolerance of the landowner

Leave Kirkwall by the A960 and continue past the tiny airport. Take the next left turn, signposted Tankerness. Follow the quiet, narrow road and pass to the right of the Loch of Tankerness, where a swan marshals her cygnets. Drive on past the old mill, which still has its water wheel. Just beyond, and to the right, stands the castellated Hall of Tankerness. Built in the 19th century, it stands on the site of a 12th-century Viking drinking hall. From 1630 until the early years of this century it was the home of the Baikie family — their town house can be visited in Walk 8.

Continue along Tankerness Hall Road to its end and park in the lay-by close to Rerwick Farm. Pass through the red kissing-gate to walk the grassy track that swings left towards the shore. The remains of the Second World War's coastal defences stand forlornly about the headland, overlooking the channel between Tankerness and the island of Shapinsay.

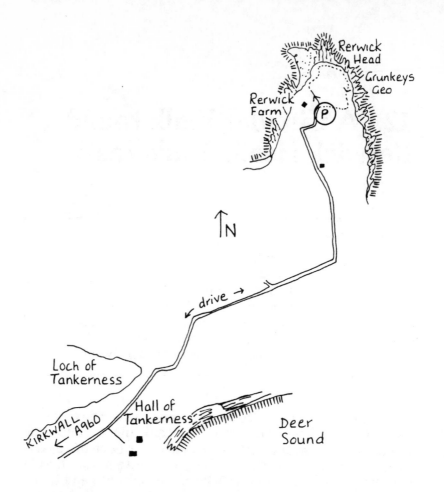

Wander round this glorious coastline. If the tide is suitable, clamber over the great sandstone flags. Notice the innumerable thin layers, stacked one on top of the next. Some areas are extensive and seem flat enough to play tennis on.

Shags and eiders doze on rugged skerries. Redshanks and ringed plover call from a tangle of seaweed at the edge of a small stretch of sand. Guillemots fly round the headland and a great skua is chased off by a very angry pair of black-backed gulls. On a spikey rock just off the most distant skerry sits a large cormorant with a white lower face and chin.

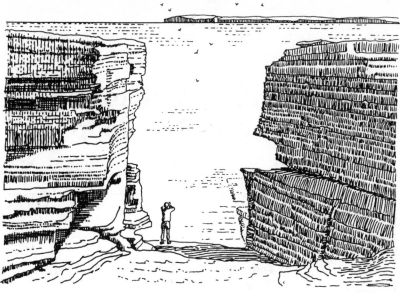

Rerwick Head

Pass a small stack, its top clad in thrift. Walk past several deep ravines where the water gurgles peacefully and then round the fenced Grunkeys Geo. Peer cautiously into them all and notice the fantastic layering of the sandstone.

Just before the last ruined building, follow the grassy track that runs inland. Here a flock of twites weave and dive over the vegetation and a house martin chases flies. Continue along the reinforced track, to the kissing-gate, to rejoin your car.

Cormorants

13. A Circular Walk to Mull Head via The Gloup

<table>
<tr><td colspan="2">Information</td></tr>
<tr><td>Distance:</td><td>4 miles</td></tr>
<tr><td>Time:</td><td>3-4 hours</td></tr>
<tr><td>Map:</td><td>Landranger 6, Pathfinder 35 Deerness, reference HY 590079 (parking)</td></tr>
<tr><td>Terrain:</td><td>Easy walking. Could be wet in parts after heavy rain. Footpaths or tracks all the way.</td></tr>
<tr><td>Status of access:</td><td>Right of way</td></tr>
</table>

Head south-west from Kirkwall on the A960 and continue on the same road through the peninsula. Follow the signpost directions for The Gloup and then for the car park at Mull Head nature reserve. Take the path for The Gloup, where a board reminds you that all dogs must be on a lead.

Walk the reed-edged path, where flower yellow vetch, buttercups and flags grow. To the right is a fine view of Copinsay, with its lighthouse, and of the cliffs of Deerness. Stand on the viewing bridge to look down into the great depths of The Gloup. This is a spectacular blow-hole, created by the action of the sea. At the landward end, the waves were brought to a sudden halt and forced upwards, causing the cave's roof to collapse in this area but leaving the seaward end intact, forming an arch or bridge. The Gloup is 40 yards long, and 80 feet deep, and the arch is 80 yards wide. Look for sea thrift and tom thumb growing on the tiny ledges of the sheer sides.

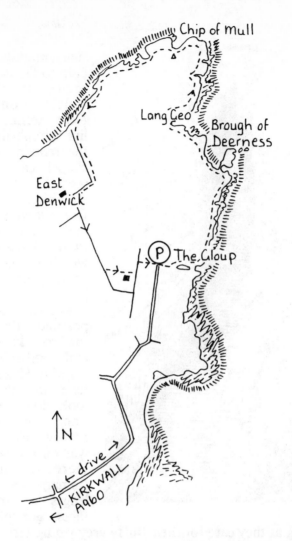

Chip of mull

Lang Geo

Brough of Deerness

East Denwick

(P) The Gloup

↑ N

← drive →

KIRKWALL A960

←

Carry on along the side of the great chasm and stand on the next viewing bridge to see the landward end of The Gloup where a tiny stream tumbles white-topped into the depths. Enjoy this magnificent natural phenomenon and then continue to the kissing-gate. Beyond, head over to the edge of the cliffs, where vast numbers of sea thrift and the delicate grass of parnassus grow. Walk on until you reach the signpost for the Brough of Deerness. Drop down the steps and then climb the

steep, muddy, narrow path to the top of the brough, the site of a Celtic monastery. Here hermit monks lived simple lives, and the remains of their chapel can still be seen. Look for seals watching curiously from the waters below and for a flock of twite dancing and wheeling over a carpet of common sorrel.

Return to the signpost and walk towards the red kissing-gate and another signpost for Mull Head. Pause here and with care look down into the Lang Geo, a long narrow chasm that was once a sea cave. Here innumerable fulmars nest on the ledges of the cliff faces, gossiping and crooning as they care for their fluffy grey youngsters.

Beyond the gate, bear left to continue along the cliff edge, which is now spangled with tormentil. Cotton grass flowers in the wetter areas and about the path flourish crowberry and lousewort. On the sea below a flock of razorbills idle in the sun. Stroll with care along the magnificent cliffs, with heather moorland stretching away to the left. The call of fulmars and the songs of pipits accompany you. As you approach the Chip of Mull, look for puffins flying in to preen on ledges just below the fulmars.

Head on along the glorious path through carpets of silver weed and with extensive views of the seemingly endless North Sea. Pass the trig point and on over moorland where two pairs of great skuas sit on rough grass and watch. Then both birds take off and dive low over the walker. Next they unsettle a colony of common gulls who set up a great cacophony.

Carry on past large purple orchis until a barbed wire fence bars your way. Turn left and stride beside it to a red kissing-gate. Beyond, walk right along a wide fenced grassy way to pass through

Silver weed

the next kissing-gate. Stroll left. (If you wish to combine this walk with Walk 14, pass through the kissing-gate on your right and walk above East Denwick. The half-mile track leads to the car park described at the start of the walk.) Continue ahead, passing through an Orkney gate of barbed wire and wooden uprights, to head up the track. From either side comes the bubbling of curlews. Overhead fly several arctic terns uttering their harsh cries although they carry sand eels dangling from their bills.

Follow the track as it swings left downhill and keep to the left of two houses. At the bottom, turn left and at the fence boundary, turn right to rejoin your car.

14. A Linear Walk to the Covenanters' Memorial

Information	
Distance:	1 mile
Time:	½-1 hour
Map:	Landranger 6, Pathfinder 35 Deerness, reference HY 582086 (parking)
Terrain:	Wide fenced grassy way. Muddy in parts after rain. Vegetation wet after rain.
Status of access:	Right of way

Leave Kirkwall by the A960 and head south-west through the peninsula. Turn left in Deerness, just after the post office and before the petrol station. Follow the signpost for the Covenanters' Memorial, a two-mile drive. Leave your car in the large parking area at the end of the narrow lane. Another signpost directs you to a long fenced track, which in high summer is lined with tall, large-headed buttercups and bird's-foot trefoil. Continue past the ruinous croft of Daisybank and walk towards the sturdy monument, erected in 1888. Pass through the red kissing-gate and walk to the foot of the memorial.

It has a panel telling the moving story of the Covenanters, who were taken prisoner at Bothwell Bridge and sent for transportation. They perished by shipwreck north-east of this point in December 1679 when the overcrowded *Crown* foundered in a storm. They were Scottish presbyterians who, in return for military aid, were allowed to introduce their form of worship

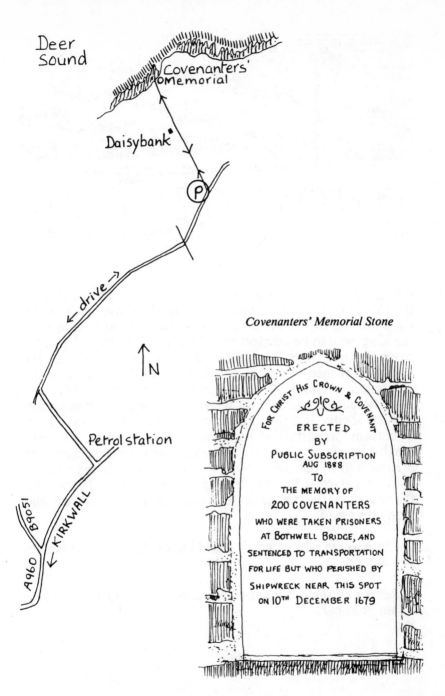

Deer Sound

Covenanters' memorial

Daisybank

P

← drive →

↑ N

Petrol station

KIRKWALL

B9051

A960

Covenanters' Memorial Stone

FOR CHRIST HIS CROWN & COVENANT

ERECTED
BY
PUBLIC SUBSCRIPTION
AUG 1888
TO
THE MEMORY OF
200 COVENANTERS
WHO WERE TAKEN PRISONERS
AT BOTHWELL BRIDGE, AND
SENTENCED TO TRANSPORTATION
FOR LIFE BUT WHO PERISHED BY
SHIPWRECK NEAR THIS SPOT
ON 10TH DECEMBER 1679

Covenanters' Memorial

into England. Later Charles II reneged on the agreement and the Covenanters were savagely persecuted. At the battle on the banks of the Clyde, those prisoners who refused to submit to the king were to be transported. Two hundred and fifty-seven manacled men were taken to Leith dock and loaded onto the ship, which then sailed round the north of Scotland to avoid any rescue attempts. As it entered Deer Sound a gale blew up. A party that went ashore for water was advised by local people to take shelter but the captain paid no heed and sailed on. The storm forced the ship onto rocks at Scarba Taing, 300 yards north-east of the monument. The captain refused to allow the prisoners to be released from the hold, though the mate is said to have passed a key to 40 or 50 who escaped. Those who floated in on wreckage were forced back into the sea and many drowned.

Close to the monument is a grid identifying the land masses you can see.

Return by the red kissing-gate and the long grassy track to rejoin your car.

15. A Circular Walk from Newark Bay via Aikerskaill

Information

Distance:	4 miles
Time:	2-3 hours
Map:	Landranger 6, Pathfinder 35 Deerness, reference HY 568042 (parking)
Terrain:	Easy walking all the way.
Status of access:	Right of way

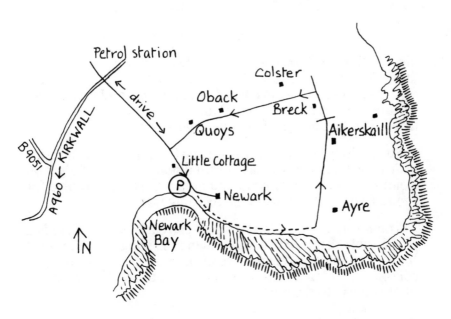

Drive as for Walk 14 to Deerness and, where you turned left after the post office and before the petrol station, turn right for this walk. Continue to the end of the narrow, quiet road and park on a grassy area just before some low dunes. Lime grass binds the sand and beyond lies the wide curving bay of Newark. On the soft grey-white sandy shore oyster-catcher, redshank and ringed plover probe, and bobbing on the water is an extended eider family, its members quietly cooing to each other.

Walk left, east, to join the waymarked public footpath to Aikerskaill Road. From this wide grassy track there are extensive views to Copinsay and its lighthouse, which is perched on

Views to Copinsay Lighthouse

high vertical cliffs facing the North Sea. Close by are its satellites, Corn Holm, Black Holm and Ward Holm. The RSPB owns the group of islands, which is known as the James Fisher Memorial Reserve. The main island can be reached by boat and details can be obtained from the Tourist Board.

Stroll along the track, which is now banked on either side with a great mass of sea mayweed. Fulmars, from the ledges on Point of Ayre, fly overhead and arctic terns dip and dive for food. Two seals peer from the receding tide.

The lovely track ends at a small car park, where there is a picnic table. Turn left to walk inland, striding the reinforced track. It joins a tarmacked road at Ayre Farm, where you continue in the same direction. Look left to see the mountains of Hoy away to the west.

Pass Aikerskaill Farm, with its black and white, double-horned Jacob sheep. Ignore the Pool turn and stroll on to pass Breck Farm. Beyond, turn left to walk a long straight road, quite traffic-free. Pass Colster with the curious carved model violin supporting its name.

Orkney vole

As you walk, watch for a creature like a small dark-brown furry pencil dashing across the road — the Orkney vole. Continue past Oback, where the pleasing smell of peat emanates from its chimney stack. At Quoys the attractive gardens catch your eye. Look for the small bales of hay stacked in a triangular shape and for the sturdy beef cattle, each farm with its own large bull.

At the T-junction, turn left again. Here in a pasture a vast flock of curlew feed and in another, large numbers of oystercatcher sit, all facing the same direction. Dawdle on past the Little Cottage and along the narrow road to rejoin your car.

16. A Circular Walk from the Village of Burray

<table>
<tr><td colspan="2">Information</td></tr>
<tr><td>Distance:</td><td>7 miles</td></tr>
<tr><td>Time:</td><td>3 hours</td></tr>
<tr><td>Map:</td><td>Landranger 7, Pathfinder 37 St Margaret's Hope, reference ND 473955 (parking)</td></tr>
<tr><td>Terrain:</td><td>Easy walking but bridleway and part of the island can be wet. Boots advisable.</td></tr>
<tr><td>Status of access:</td><td>Path by tolerance of landowner</td></tr>
</table>

Leave Kirkwall by the A961 and drive to the picturesque village of St Mary's. The village has an esplanade facing south, which was developed in the herring fishing days. Almost the last building on the right, as you leave, is a charming old storehouse with a steep roof and corbie step gables.

Beyond St Mary's, turn right to cross the first of four Churchill barriers, named after Sir Winston Churchill. These were constructed, partly by Italian prisoners-of-war, after a German submarine managed to enter Scapa Flow and torpedo *HMS Royal Oak* in October 1939, with the loss of more than 800 lives. It had manoeuvred between the old blockships.

Roads were constructed over the barriers after the war. The road over barrier 1 links Holm with Lamb Holm, where the Italian chapel stands, a poignant memorial to 550 prisoners captured during the North African campaign. Go inside

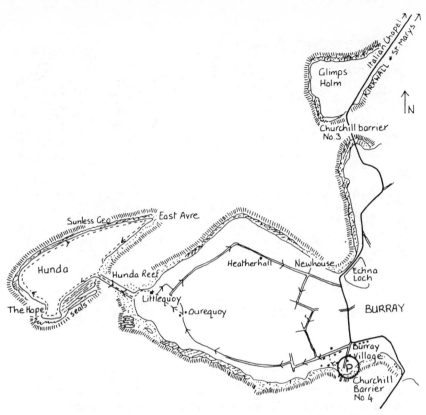

and wonder at the ingenuity of the work. Domenico Chiochetti, with the help of his fellow prisoners, transformed two
corrugated-iron nissen huts into a beautiful chapel. In 1960
Chiochetti returned to help restore the paint-work of the interior.

Continue over barrier 2 to cross Glimps Holm, and then
barrier 3, over the Weddel Sound, onto Burray. Follow the
signs for Burray village and park near the pier. The village was
another small herring station at the end of the 19th century.

Walk back past the boatyard and along the road as it swings
right, inland. Turn left along the reinforced track, with the sound
to your left and picturesque cottages to your right. Turn right at
the tarmac turning area and go across the green area seen between
the two houses. Climb the slope to a paved gap in the boundary
wall and continue to the road, where you turn left to walk the
narrow road. Where the latter swings right, carry on ahead.

Italian Chapel

Follow it as it makes a dog-leg turn, swinging right and then left. The traffic-free road takes you between fields of hay and pastures with cattle. Oyster-catchers, curlews and green plovers probe the turf for insects.

The banks of the narrow road are lined with crowberry and heather, and there is a glorious view across Water Sound to St Margaret's Hope, visited in Walk 17. Many meadow brown butterflies flit from flower to flower and several small blues sunbathe on flowering grasses. Then the island of Hoy comes into view. Where the road ends, continue along the gated

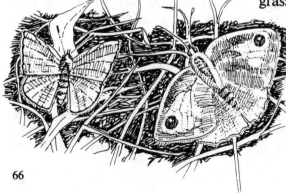

Common blue (left)
meadow brown (right)

bridleway, which is rather wet in places if there has been much rain.

The island of Hunda can then be seen. Beyond the next gate the grassy track, much drier, crosses a wide greensward that sweeps down to the sea. Flotta, Fara and Cava lie across Scapa Flow. Across Water Sound you can now see the Dam of Hoxa (Walk 17) and then to the right Wideford Hill (Walk 7) lies in the distance.

At the deserted croft of Ourequoy, stride ahead between two barns. Walk the grassy track, with a fence to your left, passing through two gates to Littlequoy. The track brings you to the yard of the farm, where George Rouse and Stephane Jaeger are delighted to welcome you and allow you through their yard to obtain access to Hunda. Stephane keeps many cashmere goats, who cry like an injured child, and here dogs should be kept on a leash at all times.

From the farm, the track leads to the causeway built on Hunda Reef. Look left to see the Sound of Hoxa. At either end of the barrier innumerable seals sing and sunbathe. Close beside the wide straight way lies a seaweed garden and overhead fly a small flock of redshank. Pass through the gate on the causeway and turn left to walk along the cliff edge, where fulmars nest. In the breeding season, herring gulls, common gulls, arctic terns and both the skuas nest on the higher moorland away from the shore, so you are asked to keep to the cliff edge and not to disturb the birds.

Keep inside the first fence and then continue along the sheep trod. The cliffs, the boulders and the shore are a glorious rich red. Crowberry, heather and bog cotton grow about the top and both the black-backed gulls fly overhead. Look across to the south to see the mountains of Caithness — a grey smudge on the horizon.

Press on round The Hope, where sea thrift carpets the cliffs and ringed plovers race over the seaweed. A group of shags snooze on projecting rocks. Hoodies fly over the heather.

Then Mainland and Kirkwall come into view. Take care on the steeper cliffs. Next you can see St Mary's across the glassy sea. Here a pair of ravens fly over the island, croaking to each other as they go. Pass the Sunless Geo, where roseroot and thrift grow on ledges where they can. As you walk on, the Churchill barrier can be seen. At East Ayre the narrow trod winds south and you can see the Hunda causeway.

From now on the indistinct path becomes rather boggy, so pick your way with care. A flock of twite, dancing and wheeling, descend on a large patch of thistles. Cross the causeway and then follow the track to return through the farmyard. Beyond, take the farm access track left and then right to join the metalled road. Walk left on the road to climb the hill. Look back to see the unbelievably beautiful view.

At the top of the slope you can see Copinsay lighthouse. Continue past the dwellings Heather Hill, Heather Hall and Klondyke. From this narrow quiet road you can see Echnaloch, separated from the sea by an ayre, over which the road runs. Turn right, opposite a house named Newhouse, to walk the steadily ascending bridleway. Turn left, where peat smoke fills the air. At the end of the track, turn right to begin the descent towards Burray village. From here you can see the Sands of Wright (Walk 17), Caithness and barrier number 4.

At the T-junction, turn left and walk through the village. Turn right towards the pier to rejoin your car.

Please call at Littlequoy as you pass.

17. A Circular Walk from the Dam of Hoxa via St Margaret's Hope, South Ronaldsay

Information

Distance:	4 miles
Time:	2-3 hours, depending on the weather
Map:	Landranger 7, Pathfinder 37 St Margaret's Hope, reference ND 431940 (parking)
Terrain:	Easy walking all the way.
Status of access:	Right of way

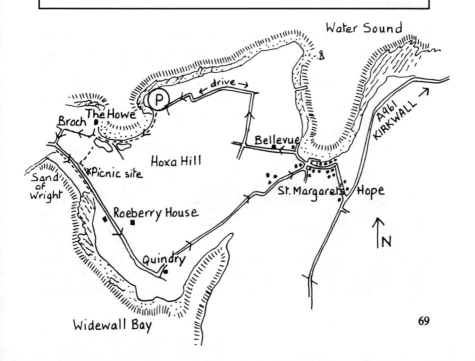

69

St Margaret's Hope

To reach South Ronaldsay, drive across the four Churchill barriers (see Walk 16). Continue into the village of St Margaret's Hope, and take the second left, to Bellevue, and drive to the end of the road. There is a good lay-by for parking and turning. A signpost directs you along the public path to Hoxa.

Walk down the concrete track towards the shore, and then bear left to walk above the lovely sandy bay, which is backed by a shingle beach. Here grow a great variety of colourful flowers. Oyster-catcher, curlew, redshank and ringed plover feed along the shoreline. Pass a small croft, which has a turf roof and a splendid kiln attached.

To the left lies a marsh with great clumps of reed, flags and some water dropwort. Next to it is a large lagoon from which rises a heron, disturbed from catching eels. Behind the lagoon is more marsh. Once these three areas were one.

Heron

To the right stands a sturdy house, The Howe, and behind are the remains of a quite substantial broch. You can still see the walls, partitions and traces of steps that would have led to a higher level. Here Earl Thorfinn Skull-Splitter, according to the Orkney saga, was buried in the 10th century. Ask the owner of the house if you can view.

At the footpath sign, turn left and then continue along the unclassified road. Climb the hill, from where you can see Widewall Bay on one side and Water Sound on the other.

Turn left to join the tarmacked road and at the T-junction turn left to walk beside the Sand of Wright. From this lovely stretch of white sand you can see South Walls and Cantick Head, the isle of Stroma, the Pentland Firth and Caithness beyond. Behind the sands is another shingle beach and it and the Dam of Hoxa enclose the lagoons and marsh seen earlier.

Fulmars nest on the cliffs on either side of the bay and eider nest in the vicinity and bring their ducklings into the sea. Oyster-catcher, snipe, curlew and redshank breed close by. Arctic terns, which also nest here, fish in the bay.

On these sands the boys of the area take part in a ploughing match with the same rules as their fathers observe in their matches. In the past the ploughs were quite simple — a cow's hoof on a stick for instance. Today the ploughs are often miniature ones, handed down through the generations. Before the competition takes place the boys, and girls as well, dress up as horses and parade through St Margaret's Hope. The parade has taken place for the last 80 years and some of the beautiful ornamental costumes are passed down.

If you spend a long time on the lovely beach, you can curtail your walk by strolling along the grassy track that passes between the lagoon and the marshy area. To do this, with your back to the bay, take the track to the left of the wire fence to the left of the excellent facilities (toilets, waiting room, picnic table, information panel). At the shore, turn right to rejoin your car.

If you wish to continue, stride up the hill to walk past the elegant Roeberry House. Then drop downhill with Widewall Bay to the right. At Quindry, the road swings sharp left and from here you can see the Oyce of Quindry and its Long Ayre. At low tide you can use it to cross to the opposite shore.

Continue along the road to St Margaret's Hope. The village is named after an early saint, Margaret, a seven-year-old princess from Norway. She died here in 1290, while on her way to marry the Prince of Wales, son of Edward I of England. The picturesque village nestles round a sheltered harbour and there is a small busy pier. Before you leave the pleasing village, visit the old forge, which has a very good display of implements used when the village had a smithy and a blacksmith. It has also a collection of photographs and letters relating to the herring industry that once occupied the villagers.

Leave by the turn to Bellevue, which you drove along earlier. Climb the hill to leave the houses behind. Follow the road right to walk where clover and moss grow down the middle. Here linnets flit about the fence posts and the wire. Continue along the quiet road as it twists and turns, finally descending to the car park.

18. A Circular Walk to see the Tomb of Eagles, South Ronaldsay

Information

Distance:	1 mile
Time:	1½ hours
Map:	Not needed for walk, Landranger 7, reference ND 464839 (parking)
Terrain:	Easy walking.
Status of access:	Path by tolerance of landowner

Drive south through South Ronaldsay. At the T-junction where you would turn right for Burwick Pier, turn left, following the signs for the Tomb of Eagles at Liddel Farm. Leave your car in the large parking area. Visit the small museum, where you are given a short lively talk and encouraged to handle skulls, eagle claws, fragments of fascinating pottery, and beads.

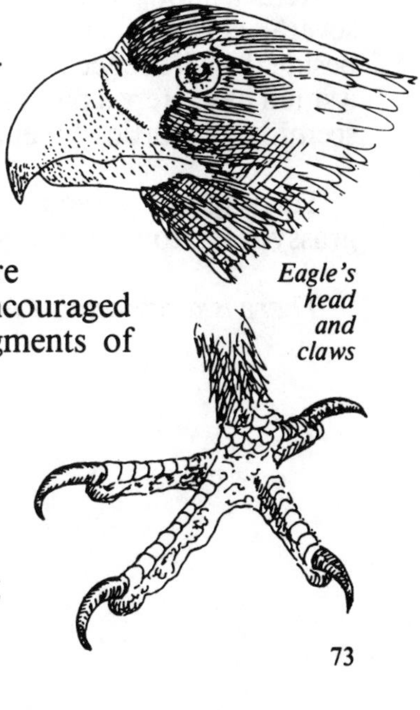

After being provided with wellingtons if necessary, you set off along a fenced grassy track to the left of the farm. It brings you to the remains of a bronze age dwelling

Eagle's head and claws

73

(1500-500 BC). Ronald Simison, the farmer, who excavated the site, gives you a fascinating talk and shows you, among other items, the large stone trough to which hot stones were continually added to heat the water for cooking food. Again you are encouraged to hold various stone artefacts and to wander around.

From here, continue along another fenced track, which brings you to the edge of cliffs composed of innumerable thin flags of sandstone. Here fulmars nest, and the way is a mass of thrift with roseroot growing in the crevices of the cliff face. The path leads to the chambered tomb.

To enter you can either crawl on hands and knees using kneeling pads and hand pads, or lie on a sturdy trolley and propel yourself along a low ceilinged passage. At the end is a surprisingly spacious stone chamber with upright slabs of stone providing partitioning. There are several small cells and shelves. Human bones, fish bones, seeds, pottery and the remains of white sea eagles were found here. The tomb is thought to have been used from 3500 to 2400 BC. After that time the top was taken off and it was deliberately filled in.

Return along the cliff edge, with magnificent views into several geos. Where the fenced track turns right, continue beside the wire fence to walk along the cliffs of the north side of a small bay. Here a pair of graceful arctic skuas dive and wheel, seemingly effortlessly, enjoying the off-shore breeze.

Turn right at the end of the bay and then left to walk another grassy track to return to your car.

There is a reasonable entrance fee. Usual concessions.

19. Two Short Walks in the RSPB's Hobbister Nature Reserve

Information

Distance:	1 mile and ½ mile
Time:	1 hour
Map:	Landranger 7, Pathfinder 34 Scapa Bay, reference HY 395069, HY382066 (parking)
Terrain:	Easy walking. Paths could be muddy after rain.
Status of access:	Path over RSPB land

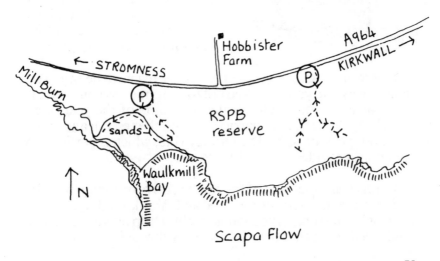

The reserve lies off the A964, four miles south-west of Kirkwall. There is a small parking area with an information board on the south side of the road, just before the turn for Waulkmill Bay.

The 1,875 acres of the Hobbister reserve are leased to the RSPB by James Grant & Co. Highland Park distillery (Walk 10), who retain peat cutting rights. Walk the old peat track between banks of heather, crowberry and wood rush. Look back for a delightful view of Loch of Kirbister and the fertile pastures of Mainland. Look ahead to see Scapa Flow.

In the wet areas among the heather moorland, yellow flags, meadow sweet and purple orchis flower, and willow grows in clumps. Where the track divides, walk left for a good view of Waulkmill Bay. Take care as you approach the cliffs of Roo Point, where fulmars and a pair of ravens are nesting.

Ravens

Return to the division of the path and take the right fork. As you walk through the heather banks, listen for the hum of an immense number of insects. Look for meadow pipits, skylarks and twites flitting about the moorland plants.

Where the track swings right, you have reached the end of the right of way and you are asked not to continue. As you return to your car park you might, at the right time of the year, see a merlin or a kestrel. Hen harriers nest on the reserve and short-eared owls can be seen. The Orkney vole, which is particularly common, provides food for these birds-of-prey.

To reach another part of the reserve, drive on along the A964 and take the next left turn, signposted Waulkmill Bay. Park in the first lay-by (unmarked) on the right. Drop down the narrow reinforced track that descends steadily through heather to the

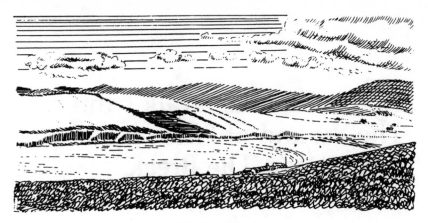

Waulkmill Bay

edge of the glorious sands. Continue along the bay to the estuary of Mill Burn. Here shelduck, arctic terns, redshank, oyster-catchers and common gulls feed. The sands are extensive and a delightful place to idle and beachcomb.

Return along the shoreline. As you climb the steps to rejoin your car, look for a pair of stonechats perched atop a bushy heather plant.

20. A Circular Walk from The Bu and St Nicholas's Church via The Breck

Information	
Distance:	2 miles
Time:	1 hour
Map:	Landranger 7, Pathfinder 33 Stromness and the Old Man of Hoy, reference HY 335045 (parking)
Terrain:	Easy walking.
Status of access:	Path created by agreement

Drive south-west from Kirkwall on the A964 and after some 8 miles, turn left on the road to Gyre. Park close to St Nicholas's Church. Here, in a sycamore, a wren scolds a small grey cat that gets too near to its nest. Walk up the well-kept grassy way, which is bordered with whitebeam, sycamore and rowan, to two information panels.

One of the panels explains that The Bu, a manor house of the Norse Earls of Orkney in the 12th century, was built to the north side of the church. It comprised a group of farm buildings, a drinking hall for feasting and other store rooms and chambers. The stones and foundations you can see to the left of the path may have formed part of that complex.

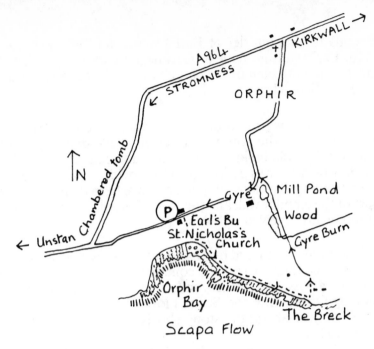

Pass through the kissing-gate to view the remains of the round church, which the panel claims is almost certainly the church mentioned in the *Orkneyinga Saga,* composed in 1136. It is thought to have been built by Earl Hakon Paulson to make

Orphir Church

amends for the murder of Earl Magnus on Egilsay in about 1116. Earl Paulson made a pilgrimage to Jerusalem after the murder and the plan of the church may have been inspired by the Holy Sepulchre.

The church was used until 1705 when a new building was constructed to the south-west, partly embodying the older building. The old building was used as a storage shed until 1756 when two-thirds was pulled down to provide stone to repair the later building. The later church has since been demolished and part of the circular wall and the apse of the old church has been dramatically revealed.

Leave the churchyard by a hand gate in the east wall and walk towards the shore. Cross the concrete footbridge over a small beck to a kissing-gate. Beyond, stroll along the cliffs over-looking Orphir Bay and Scapa Flow. Walk with the fence to your left just above the stony shore, with spectacular views over to Hoy.

Beyond the second pasture, the way continues inside the wall where the sea has eroded the cliffs. Press on along the sward of the low cliffs, where a multitude of flowers colour the way. Fulmars, shags, greater black-backed gulls and great skuas fly overhead. Redshanks and oyster-catchers feed on the shoreline.

Carry on through the heather, crowberry and low-growing willow. Look for degutted sea urchins and dead starfish, the remains of some predator's feast. Continue to the area known as The Breck and to two stone-built fishermen's huts. Look for a natural gully that might have been a slipway down to a tiny bay and for hollows (nousts) where the boats would have lain, close to the huts.

From the huts, bear left, to follow a narrow path inland, keeping to the right of a small burn. Pass a derelict stone cottage to join an access track which heads in the same direction. At the tarmacked road, turn left, then follow it as it swings inland. Here the road is hedged with gorse and low-growing sycamore.

Away to the right you can see Swanbister Bay. In the marshland nearer the road a huge flock of curlew feed. Continue uphill to walk beside the Gyre Burn, which is almost hidden by yellow flags, false watercress and forget-me-nots. Then stroll on past woodland where sycamore, ash, rowan and wych elm flourish. From the depth of the trees comes the song of a wren.

Head on along the road lined with pink purslane and honeysuckle. Gorse forms a hedge on either side. Ignore the left turn and stride on past a small lake, once a mill pond, colonised by reeds where mallards swim. At the road junction, turn

Pink purslane

left and walk the quiet narrow road, which is edged with low-growing elderberry and beech. Continue past Gyre, a house with a crenellated tower, to return to your car.

While in this part of Mainland you might wish to drive towards Stromness to visit the Unstan chambered tomb. It is signposted off the A965 and lies back from the road, behind a cottage. The stone tomb, which dates from about 3500 to 3000 BC, has lost its original roof but inside, reached by a low passage, is a large oval chamber. This is partitioned into five compartments by upright slabs of stone and there is one cell with a sturdy lintel that carries Norse runes and the carving of a bird.

During excavation in 1884, the remains of skeletons were found, including two crouched skeletons in the side cell. Pottery found was of the type known as Unstan ware.

21. A very short Walk at Lochside Viewpoint, Loch of Harray

Information

Distance:	½ mile
Time:	½ hour
Map:	Landranger 7, Pathfinder 31 Finstown, reference HY 314134 (parking)
Terrain:	Easy walking, but can be very wet in parts.
Status of access:	Path created by agreement

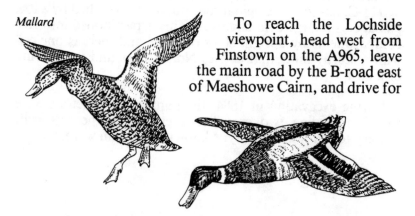

Mallard

To reach the Lochside viewpoint, head west from Finstown on the A965, leave the main road by the B-road east of Maeshowe Cairn, and drive for half a mile to the parking area. From here you can look over the Loch of Harray to see the Ring of Brodgar and, beyond, the Loch of Stenness. Both lochs are designated Sites of Special

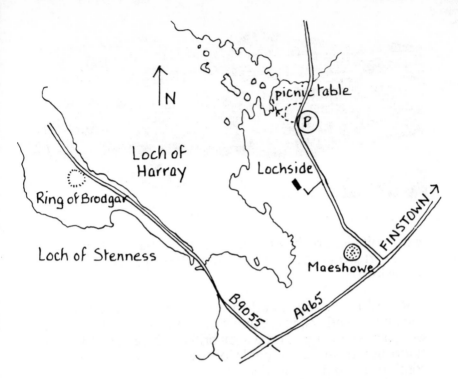

Scientific Interest (SSSIs) because their waters range from a salinity close to that of sea water through to fresh water and because of their associated wildlife and plants. The lochs contain sea and brown trout and in winter hold large flocks of pochard, tufted duck, goldeneye, mallard, widgeon and mute swan.

Leave the parking area and walk down the grassy path towards the picnic table, through a colourful carpet of heather and hawkweed. Across the tiny bay is a large stand of reeds from where comes the erratic song of a sedge warbler. Walk left across the duckboarding to the stile, passing a mass of meadow sweet, forget-me-not, milkmaid, marsh stitchwort, yellow flag, bog cotton, marsh cinquefoil, spearwort, water mint, water dropwort and ragged robin.

A pair of red-throated divers fly in uttering their haunting calls. A flock of tufted duck idle on the water, giving their soft liquid song. Beyond the stile, walk right to pass more open

83

Lochside Viewpoint

water colonised by bog bean. Cross a wet patch where marsh lousewort grows and then climb the little slope for a good view of the loch.

Return to the stile and then walk right, through hay rattle and all the heathers, in the direction of the shore. This is a very wet part where a great mass of brilliant blue forget-me-nots flourishes. If you have suitable footwear, cross the wet area and continue on to the loch edge.

Return to your car by the same route.

22. A Linear Walk from Swartland to Russland Road

<table>
<tr><td colspan="2">Information</td></tr>
<tr><td>Distance:</td><td>4 miles, if you return along the track</td></tr>
<tr><td>Time:</td><td>2 hours</td></tr>
<tr><td>Map:</td><td>Landranger 6, Pathfinder 28 Dounby and 31 Finstown, reference HY 275209 (parking)</td></tr>
<tr><td>Terrain:</td><td>Easy walking, but can be muddy. Stout shoes advisable.</td></tr>
<tr><td>Status of access:</td><td>Right of way</td></tr>
</table>

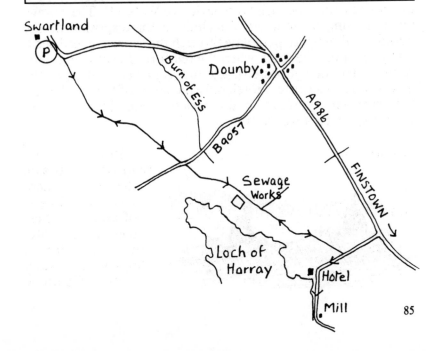

Park at the start of the signposted footpath, near Swartland, which is reached by a narrow road leading west from Dounby. The wide fenced track leads through the agricultural heart of Orkney. Fields of hay and barley border the way and in pastures beef cattle graze.

Flocks of curlew feed where the hay has been removed. Green plovers wheel and call as they fly overhead. Oyster-catchers set up a perpetual background of piping. Young meadow pipits sit on fence posts and then chase each other up the track.

The way is flower-lined and a joy to walk. Away to the right rear the dramatic tops of the hills of Hoy, and to the left loom the brooding heather-clad hills of north-east Mainland. Pass through the red-stained kissing-gates to reach the B9057, which you cross. To the right stand the Decca pylons, a navigational system for ships.

Stride on along the continuing track through more quiet pastures. The Loch of Harray comes into view. On its shore stands a new sewage plant. Just before the landscaped site, join the reinforced, wide track that passes over a narrow fast-flowing stream. The loch is an SSSI (see Walk 21). The sewage plant is using an innovative technique for disposing of the outfall. It allows it to percolate through the extensive reed beds. Carry on along the track when the reinforced way swings left. At the end of the signposted track, turn right and walk down the quiet road to Merkister Hotel, once the home of Eric Linklater, the writer. Here you can obtain a welcome cup of tea or coffee, or perhaps even a wee dram.

Fishermen

Follow the quiet road as it runs beside the loch, where you can see dozens of swans. Fishermen sit patiently in their boats hoping to catch trout. Continue to the disused Harray Mill. This traditionally built 19th-century parish meal mill is peculiar in that before 1875 it did not possess a drying kiln. Farmers wishing to make use of it had to dry their own barley and oats before taking them for milling.

This is the place to be picked up; or maybe at the hotel. If you do not have transport awaiting you, return by the same footpath to rejoin your car.

If you have a friend who will drop you at Swartland and pick you up at the Merkister Hotel or the Harray Mill, Russland, you can combine this linear walk with a visit to Maeshowe Cairn, Tormiston Mill, Stones of Stenness and the Ring of Brodgar.

Ring of Brodgar

23. A Walk through Stromness

Information	
Distance:	½-1 mile
Time:	2-3 hours
Map:	The Heritage Guide produced by Stromness Community Council; Landranger 6, Pathfinder 33 Stromness and the Old Man of Hoy, reference HY 255095 (parking)
Terrain:	Beware of unexpected traffic along the cobbled and flagged main street.
Status of access:	Right of way

Park at the north end, the 'younger' end, of Stromness. Close to the long stay car park is a fine house known as Speddings (1). It has two interesting arches in its ground floor and a long flight of steps up to the main house. Long before the A965 was built, the tide must have washed the side of the house.

Stroll on past the Speddings, with the sheltered, deep-water harbour (2) to your left. Enjoy the activity, as varied and busy today as it has always been. In the 18th century, war brought prosperity to the harbour, followed, in the 19th century, by expanding trade, boat-building and repairs, and a herring boom. During the 20th century, war again kept Stromness harbour busy. In the First World War, Stromness was one of the headquarters of the Royal Navy. In the Second World War it supported the navy at Scapa Flow. Today the roll-on, roll-off ferries come into the harbour and it has a substantial fishing industry.

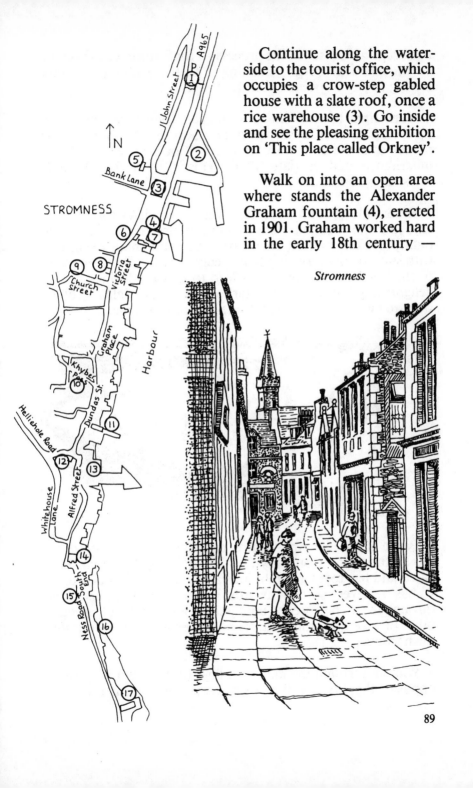

Continue along the waterside to the tourist office, which occupies a crow-step gabled house with a slate roof, once a rice warehouse (3). Go inside and see the pleasing exhibition on 'This place called Orkney'.

Walk on into an open area where stands the Alexander Graham fountain (4), erected in 1901. Graham worked hard in the early 18th century —

Stromness

bankrupting himself in the process — for Stromness to become an independent burgh, enabling it to trade abroad without having to pay a special tax to Kirkwall.

Turn right to walk into the flagged John Street and then up a sloping alley towards Millar's House (5). Look for the plaque over the door with the words 'God's providence is my inheritance' and the date '1716'. This is the earliest dateable house in Stromness.

Return along John Street and wander down Victoria Street, enjoying the pleasant vista of flagged streets (6), lined with tightly packed houses, many of which are small businesses with shop fronts surviving from years gone by. Between many of the buildings narrow alleys lead to small moorings, giving delightful glimpses of the harbour. On the right, cobbled stepped closes lead up the hillside of Brinkies Brae.

Herring boats

Pause at the Pier Arts Centre, once the recruiting centre for the Hudson Bay Company (7). The building has been renovated and has regular exhibitions and a children's workroom. It has received several awards and commendations. Pass through the arch to see the boat jetty beyond and look along to other picturesque stone jetties and the extensive view out into the harbour.

Wander through the maze of alleys (8) that climb up right, opposite the Lounge Bar, and weave left to enter Church

Street (9). The aptly named street, often called Kirk Road, has three churches in 200 yards. Can you spot them?

Continue into Graham Place, where cobbles run through the middle of large flags. On the sea side lived Alexander Graham (see 4). A small row of houses was demolished here to help the traffic flow.

Beyond Graham Place, walk on through the narrowing main street to see the Khyber Pass (10), a narrow stepped alley that linked the houses on the banks with the jetties.

Carry on to pass the lifeboat station (11). And then a wider area is reached where Alfred Street joins Dundas Street and Helliehole Road. On the corner of the latter is Stromness library (12), built in 1905.

Look for the large premises that house the Northern Lighthouse depot (13), once another part of the Hudson Bay Company. Part of the building replicates the living quarters found at the foot of lighthouses.

Continue along the attractive Alfred Street to the museum (14), housed in the old town hall. Find time to enjoy the interesting displays. Here much of the life of the Hudson Bay Company's employees is revealed. The museum has a good natural history display and a section on the days of sail. There is a small entry fee.

Follow the quiet way (choose Thursday — early closing day) into the older end of the town. Login's well (15) lies to the right. Peer through a window to see the plethora of ferns thriving within. This well watered the Hudson Bay Company's ships from 1670 to 1891. Captain Cook's ships, Sir John Franklin's and the merchant vessels of earlier years all used the well. It was sealed up in 1931.

Head on along the paved way, now South End, which runs into Ness Road. Here the flagstones cease. Sit on Stanger's Brae (16), beside the cannon, and enjoy the magnificent sea and landscape. The gun was fired on the arrival in harbour of the Hudson Bay Company ships. Look right to see a charming house (17), which looks like two. Here lived a Mrs. Christian Robertson, a redoubtable lady who, as shipping agent, employed hundreds of men to sail the whaling boats.

To rejoin your car, return through the conservation area, which has preserved the character of Stromness for the enjoyment of residents, visitors and future generations.

24. A Circular Walk via the Shore south-west of Stromness

Information

Distance:	4 miles
Time:	2 hours
Map:	Landranger 6, Pathfinder 33 Stromness and the Old Man of Hoy, reference HY 235086 (parking)
Terrain:	Easy walking all the way.
Status of access:	Path created by agreement/Right of way

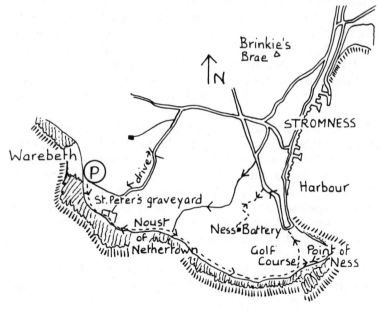

Hoy Sound

St Peter's graveyard

Leave Stromness by the Back Road. Bear right in the direction of Innertown and then follow the directions for Warebeth Beach. Turn right at St Peter's graveyard and continue along a track to park above the beach.

Walk the narrow path above the shore, in the direction of the graveyard. Below, on the skerries (long ledges of red sandstone tilting into the sea), small families of eider preen. Black-backed gulls and a great skua glide overhead and redshanks fly restlessly from one rock ridge to another, uttering their haunting call. Ringed plover run in and out of the water as the tide gently recedes. A flock of starlings noisily peck at a clump of seaweed.

The path is lined with thrift, pink campion, eyebright, yellow bedstraw, pink clover, sea mayweed and hawkbit. Across Hoy Sound you have a wonderful view of the mountains of Hoy — the tops of Ward Hill, Cuilags and its magnificent cliffs occasionally veiled in mist. You can look up the Burra Sound, between Graemsay and Hoy, to see the boats carrying amateur divers circling the blockship *The Inverlaine*. The boat struck a mine in 1941 and was sunk here in 1944.

Pass through a red kissing-gate to walk beside the graveyard wall, where pied wagtails flit from stone to stone. Look

over the wall to see an interesting 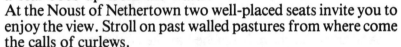 *Oyster-catchers*
carved stone on
the remains of an
old chapel.

Stride along the
pleasing path.
Graemsay's light-
houses, Hoy High and
Hoy Low, lie across the
Sound. Oyster-catchers and
hoodies feed on the shore and
a seal bobs up from the water.
At the Noust of Nethertown two well-placed seats invite you to
enjoy the view. Stroll on past walled pastures from where come
the calls of curlews.

Where the track divides, continue ahead above the shore. Here
meadow pipits flit about above the grassy sward. At the metalled
road, carry on below the golf course. Walk beside the picnic site
on your right and head on to Point of Ness. Sea rocket grows on
the shore and there is a magnificent view across to Ophir and
out over the waters of Scapa Flow. The old gun batteries which
protected Stromness have been reinstated and an information
board explains Scapa Flow's importance through history.

Return the 50 yards of the Ness and turn right to walk the
narrow road beside the east side of the golf course. Climb through
Guardhouse Park estate and walk on to turn left at the footpath
sign for the Gun Viewpoint. Follow the next footpath sign left
and walk to the large outcrop of rock from which Stromness pilots
once watched for boats approaching from the west or east, through
the south isles, to avoid the dangerous tides of the Pentland Firth.

An information panel says that, during the 18th and early 19th
centuries, international shipping avoided the war-torn English
Channel by sailing around the north of Scotland. The many boats
awaiting a fair wind, both at Longhope and Cairston, provided
constant work for local pilots and boatmen. In 1821 Stromness
had 26 licensed pilots, more than any other Scottish port.

The gun after which the viewpoint is named was a 32-pounder cannon mounted there before the First World War. In 1941 the army removed it to make room for an anti-aircraft gun emplacement to defend Scapa Flow. The cannon was used as scrap to help the war effort. Today the mound is topped with a 360-degrees viewfinder to help you identify the spectacular scene.

Return to the road by the same footpath and continue left, up the hill. Turn left to walk a narrow road, passing a cottage, and then following the road through the walled pastures. Hay dries in the fields on the left and cows with young calves graze on the right. Twites wheel and dart overhead, chattering as they go.

And then the shore is reached at the Noust, with its strategically placed seat. Turn right to continue along the path to rejoin your car.

25. A Visit to Skara Brae followed by a Circular Walk

Information	
Distance:	3 miles
Time:	1 hour
Map:	Landranger 6, Pathfinder Finstown 31 and Dounby 28, reference HY 234187 (parking)
Terrain:	Easy walking all the way.
Status of access:	Path by tolerance of landowner

Skara Brae, a small village with houses and alleyways, throve on the shore of the Bay of Skaill 4,500 years ago. It gradually became choked by its own rubble and then, over the millennia, was buried under sand blown in from the magnificent bay. In about 1850, a tremendous storm ripped away the rough clay and sand dunes between the houses and the sea and exposed sturdy stone walls — some to eaves level — passageways and the stone furniture used by our neolithic ancestors.

The car park for the site lies at Skaill House. Here lived William Watt, the laird of Skaill, on whose land the site of the village lay hidden and whose trustees bequeathed it to the nation. It has been excavated several times this century.

Pass through the visitor centre and follow the signs for Skara Brae.

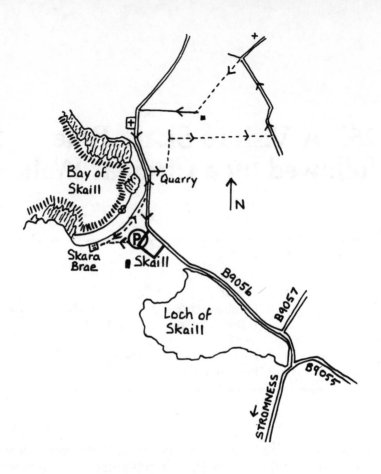

There is an admission fee, with the usual concessions. A shop sells a guide book and shows an excellent video. Numbered information boards help you to understand the excavations. House number 1 shows the basic layout of all the houses.

As you view the site, ponder on the lives of these ancient people. How did they get that gentle curve to the walls of their houses, and how were the boulders shaped and levered into place? Why build at Skara Brae? Perhaps there was a fresh-water lagoon behind the dune system? Did the people obtain their protein from the sea? Did they use the skins of beached whales and driftwood for roofing over their dwellings?

Skara Brae

As you return from this magical site, look seawards, left, at the white-topped waves breaking gently on the shore, a shore littered with jellyfish. Ringed plover race along the sand and oyster-catchers noisily feed at the water's edge.

Continue past the car park, the toilet block and the lay-by where road surfacing material is stored. Just beyond, turn right to walk a grassy cart-track. Where the way becomes gated, turn left through an Orkney gate and walk another grassy track. Ragged robin, sea mayweed, buttercups, yellow flags, bedstraw, corn marigolds and deep purple orchis flower along the way. In the wet areas thrive kingcups and forget-me-nots. Horsetails growing in profusion on either side of the track show how wet it can be.

Turn right into another grassy track, leading off by a stretch of dry-stone wall, and stride out into the peace of the gently undulating countryside. The only sounds to disturb the tranquil way are the piping of oyster-catchers and the bickering of arctic terns. Stroll on, with fields of barley or hay on either side, until you reach a narrow road, where you turn left.

Climb the steadily ascending hill to pass the turn to House-garth, and walk on where curlews call from the pastures. Look for the many Orkney gates used for giving access to these fields. At the next right turn, for Quoyloo church, turn left to walk another wide grassy track. Ahead is a magnificent view of the grassy slopes topping the cliffs above Skara Brae. Look for the natural arch, Hole o' Row, jutting into the sea. Beyond, you can see the sheer rose-pink cliffs of Hoy.

When you reach a modern cottage, turn right and walk the narrow, reinforced road to the B9056, where you turn left. On the right stands a disused church. Look in the graveyard for the enclosed graves of William Watt and his family.

Continue along the road to rejoin your car.

Orkney gate

26. A Circular Heritage Walk, Eday

<table>
<tr><td colspan="2">Information</td></tr>
<tr><td>Distance:</td><td>5 miles</td></tr>
<tr><td>Time:</td><td>3-4 hours</td></tr>
<tr><td>Map:</td><td>Heritage leaflet for walk; Landranger 5, Pathfinder 27 Sanday Sound and 24 Westray, reference HY 569367 (parking)</td></tr>
<tr><td>Ferry:</td><td>Leaves from Kirkwall several times a week. Book the day before (Telephone 01856 872044).</td></tr>
<tr><td>Status of access:</td><td>Path created by agreement</td></tr>
</table>

After leaving the ferry, bear right and, on joining the B9063, right again. Continue past the school and the church. Beyond lies London airport, with its grassy airstrip set amid heather! Drive on to park in front of Eday Community Enterprises Shop.

Walk up the narrow road opposite the shop, signposted Eday Heritage Walk. Colourful flowers edge the road and attractive ferns grow in the ditch. From here you can smell the pleasing aroma of peat smoke from the dwellings beside the shop. Beyond Mill Loch, heather covers the slopes of Resting Hill and to the left lies rough pasture where cattle feed.

Do not approach the loch but enter the excellent hide to see the birds. Several pairs of red-throated divers accompany their young. Another pair fly in and the nearest pair swim round and round the incomers, churning the water and giving them a very

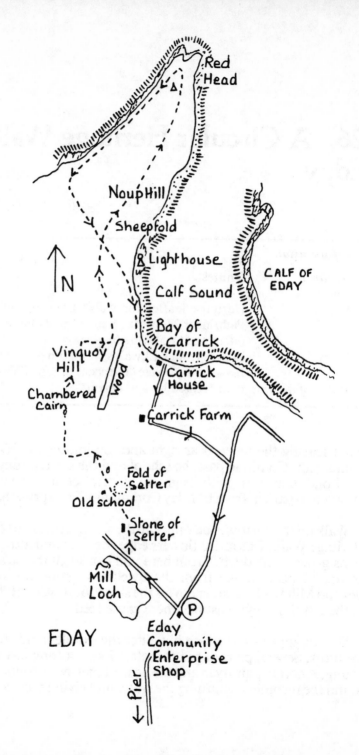

Red
Head

Noup Hill

Sheepfold

Lighthouse

Calf Sound

CALF OF
EDAY

Bay of
Carrick

N

Vinquoy
Hill

Wood

Carrick
House

Chambered
Cairn

Carrick Farm

Fold of
Setter

Old school

Stone of
Setter

Mill
Loch

P

EDAY

Eday
Community
Enterprise
Shop

Pier

Red-throated diver

noisy reception. A pair of great skuas rest on the loch and preen assiduously. A heron flies in to land on a small island close to shore and the divers in unison set up a continuous eerie wailing.

Leave the hide and walk up the road to a signposted path to the Stone of Setter, a magnificent standing stone, nearly 15 feet high and set

Stone of Setter

in a meadow of flowering grasses. It is festooned with lichen and a rough twiggy nest adorns a groove at the top. Ahead is a glorious view of the Bay of Carrick and its sands, golden in the sunshine.

Stride on beyond the waymarked kissing-gate to continue over duckboards in the direction of what looks like a barn but once was a school. Close by, try to discern a large circular walled enclosure, the remaining stones of which are covered with heather. This is known as the Fold of Setter and may be all that is left of a prehistoric enclosure for livestock. Pass over more duckboards. To the right of the next marker post is a large chambered tomb. It is now roofless but has kept a few of the massive upright slabs that divided the tomb into compartments.

Follow the waymarked posts over rough grass, where grow bedstraw and tormentil, to more heather. Here look for the Huntersquoy tomb, which once was two-storeyed, similar to Taversöe Tuick in Rousay (see Walk 31). The lower chamber is full of water, which supports a fine crop of duckweed and a garden of ferns. Little remains of the upper chamber, which had its own entrance.

Bear left to climb Vinquoy Hill. By the signpost, look right to see a neolithic turf wall. Continue climbing to the signpost on top of the ridge. It stands beside Vinquoy chambered tomb, which dates from before 2,000 BC. The tomb was a burial chamber for the local community and the central chamber has four cells opening from it. It is approached by crawling or walking crouched along a narrow passage. The red sandstone that forms the walls was probably obtained from the small quarries around the site.

The beehive-shaped tomb was restored in 1985 and a sympathetic small dome added to allow in daylight. The exquisite tomb is of the Maeshowe type and even the claustrophobic cannot fail to be amazed at the wonderful construction.

Stroll on along the ridge, where a kestrel hunts for prey. Ahead you can see the Calf of Eday in its entirety. Across to the left lies Faray and the Holm of Faray, with a storm racing up the sound. The path through the hummocks of heather and crowberry is littered with pieces of warm red sandstone. Continue to the summit cairn and the view indicator. From here on a clear day you can see the north isles and Mainland of Orkney and Fair Isle of Shetland.

Stride to the drystone wall and turn right, as directed by the signpost, to descend to Vinquoy Hill plantation. The wood is composed of stunted and twisted European larch and lodgepole pine. Newly planted alders grow in their protective sleeves. Lady fern and broad buckler fern provide a pleasant under-storey. A dense growth of gorse surrounds the plantation. Wood pigeons, hedge sparrows, chaffinches and blackbirds breed here.

Pass through a kissing-gate to continue along the side of the hill, overlooking Calf Sound with its brilliant white small lighthouse. Descend to a valley where a snipe rises, with fast whirring wings, from feeding in the ooze close to a circular sheep pen. Wheatears make full use of the drystone walled enclosure. Here two signposts give directions, one for a path over the top of Noup Hill to Red Head and the other for a route along the coast.

To ascend Noup Hill, climb straight up and continue over a dense mat of heather. Now you are level with the northern tip of the Calf, with its several dramatic natural arches, which provide ledges for a large colony of fulmars. Beyond you can see the island of Sanday.

Walk on towards the headland, where the vegetation changes to ankle-twisting tussocks of grass. Here is the trig point but the indicator panel has disappeared. Stand by the wire-fenced cliff edge to see more fulmars, together with kittiwakes, puffins and guillemots, continually flying towards, and away from, the ledges of the immensely high cliffs. Far below shags fly low across the white-topped breakers, and seals swim.

Walk west, keeping beside the sturdy fence on your right, with occasional glimpses of the sea below. Overhead half a dozen arctic skuas glide lazily, mewing quietly, until a tern appears. Then they wheel and dive and chase the tern until it disgorges the food it has caught for its young on the shore near the lighthouse. A pair of great skuas fly overhead and settle on a heather tuft.

Head on along the waymarked fence and then beside a wall that continues beyond. Here noisy oyster-catchers fly low over the moor. Swing left, following the wall, and walk an indistinct way — but take care as the heather conceals many ankle traps. Look for purple orchis here.

Drop down the slope to the two signposts seen earlier. Follow the one for Carrick House. Keep to the track that heads towards the gracious house, a 17th-century laird's dwelling built for the Earl of Carrick in 1633. Here in 1725 John Gow, the pirate (see Walk 8), was taken prisoner after grounding on the Calf of Eday. Notice the four cannon pointing out to sea.

Follow the signposts, keeping well above the shore, to a kissing-gate close to the house. Please remember this is a private house and no approach to the road should be made along the shore. Keep to the outside wall of the house and pass through a gate to the narrow road, where you turn right.

The way is bordered with salmonberry and sycamores, from where comes the song of a wren. Notice the vaccary walls that divide the pastures. Look for the glorious flowers, growing tall and lush, sheltered by the steep sides of a ditch beside the track. At the attractive home farm, turn left. Here curlews fly over the pasture, calling as they go.

Walk up the road to the T-junction, where you turn right to rejoin your car.

The Eday Heritage Walk was set up in 1986 by the Department of Planning and Museums, Orkney Islands Council.

27. A Circular Walk on the Island of Hoy via the Rackwick Footpath

Information

Distance:	9 miles
Time:	4 hours
Map:	Landranger 7, Pathfinder 33 Stromness and the Old Man of Hoy, reference HY 245039 (Moness Pier)
Terrain:	Footpath to Rackwick muddy in places. Walking boots required.
Ferry:	Foot passenger ferry leaves Stromness from the south steps, south of the P & O pier. It journeys to Moness Pier, Hoy. Pay on the boat, no return ticket. No booking required.
Status of access:	Right of way

The name Hoy means high land. After Mainland, Hoy is Orkney's largest island. The north and west of the island are very hilly, and the south is low lying and fertile.

Dolphins

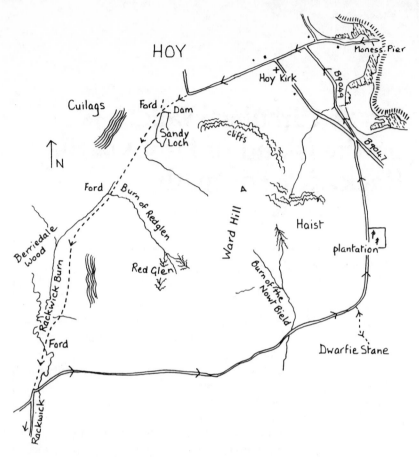

The ferry-boat, the *Jessie Ellen,* is a small and sturdy boat, and takes you speedily across Hoy Sound, where you may see a basking shark or a leaping dolphin. The ferry continues past the skerries at the entrance to Burra Sound and close to the blockship (see Walk 24). Arctic terns dive for food and great skuas fly lazily, waiting for an easy meal. Fulmars fish and float on the water. Guillemots swim close to the boat and then fly ahead with a fine display of red legs.

Walk up the road from Moness pier (good facilities here) with a dramatic view ahead of Cuilags and Ward Hill (1,570 feet). Hoy is mostly formed of Upper Old Red Sandstone, overlying the Middle Old Red Sandstone, of which much of Orkney is composed. Steep and craggy hills result.

Hoy Church

Continue ahead along the narrow road, which is lined with a glorious array of wild flowers. In pastures beside the road, hoodies, oyster-catchers, green plovers and curlews probe. To the left, high on its hill, stands Hoy Parish Church. Stride on and then glance back, right, to see a conspicuous grassy hill. This is a volcanic plug, a remnant of the lava that once flowed over the landscape.

Where the road swings right, continue ahead along the signposted Rackwick footpath. Here an information panel welcomes you to the North Hoy Nature Reserve. The path is clear to follow and has had much work done on it — footbridges, duckboarding, conveniently placed and arrowed boulders all assist you to cross the small streams. It gently climbs and gently descends through the heather moorland of the magnificent U-shaped Rackwick Valley. On the left you pass Sandy Loch, whose dammed waters flow under a sturdy bridge.

After a mile and a half, look right for Berriedale Wood, the most northerly natural woodland in Britain. Here grow aspen, rowan, birch and hazel, providing breeding sites for small birds. Towards the end of the footpath, it comes close to the Rackwick Burn, a shallow, deeply-stained, fast-flowing stream. Its banks are lined with low-growing willow and a host of water-loving plants. Ahead lies the settlement of Rackwick and the Pentland Firth. Beyond you can see the Scottish mainland, a smudge of grey on the horizon.

When you reach a steadily ascending narrow road, turn left. Enjoy the immense variety of flowers that thrive along the grassy verge. Look for field gentians, dark blue milkwort, stone bramble and frog orchid. High on Ward Hill an arctic skua is chased off by a pair of angry ravens. Carry on along the road to cross the Burn of the Nowt Bield (burn of no sheepfolds). Here in banks of heather a pair of wrens scold. Look upstream to see an armchair-shaped corrie, scoured out by a retreating glacier. To the right a burn tumbles out of its glen in a series of pretty falls.

After two miles, you come to the signpost for the Dwarfie Stane. Turn right to walk the third of a mile, on duckboards crossing wet moorland, to see Britain's only rock-cut tomb. A solitary block of red sandstone lying below the Dwarfie Hamars, it is a prehistoric tomb with a man-made passage and flanking cells. It is believed to date from about 3000 BC. The tomb was formerly sealed by the blocking stone, which now lies in front of the entrance.

Look for the interesting graffiti, much of it Victorian. One inscription is in Persian and local people tell of a Major William Mouncey, an eccentric who, after working as a spy in Persia, would dress in Persian costume and sleep in the tomb. High above on the rock ledges of the hamars, fulmars still care for their large fluffy young. Return over the duckboarding where clumps of oblong-leaved sundew grow.

At the road, turn right and head on, with a good view of Burra Sound and the island of Graemsay beyond. A resplendent male stonechat sits on a telegraph wire, on guard over its nest below in the heather. Continue past a conifer plantation. Many silvery skeletons of trees stand on the south and east sides. Close to the road birch, rowan and aspen have been planted. Whitebeam, low-growing and stunted, grows beyond.

Then the pier and the blockship come into view. At the T-junction, turn left onto the B9047, and then immediately take the right fork where the road divides. Head along the road to the next T-junction, where you turn right to return to the pier.

28. A Linear Walk to the Old Man of Hoy

Information	
Distance:	5 miles
Time:	2-3 hours
Map:	Landranger 7, Pathfinder 33 Stromness and the Old Man of Hoy, 36 Hoy (South), reference ND 200998 (parking)
Terrain:	The peat track is a pleasure to walk. There is a steady climb at the start and a little scrambling. Boots advisable.
Status of access:	Path over RSPB land

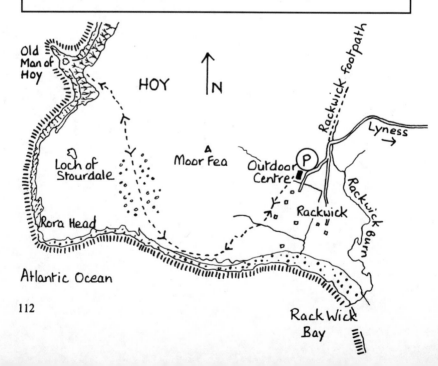

Take the roll-on roll-off ferry from Houton, which lies just off the A964, nine miles from Kirkwall and six miles from Stromness. If you are taking a vehicle, you must book in advance — the day before at the latest.

The ferry passes close to the island of Cava and then continues to Flotta, where from the pier you can see the extensive Occidental oil terminal. The boat then continues around the island of Fara to the pier at Lyness. On leaving the pier, follow the signpost for Rackwick — 13 miles along a narrow, scenic road.

Dog rose

As you near the settlement, follow the signs for the Old Man and park close to the outdoor centre. Walk the grassy path to a signposted stile, where you are asked to keep all dogs on a lead. Beyond, stride on as directed by the waymarks. The path comes to a small burn, which tumbles through a narrow ravine choked with luxuriant vegetation. Here grow rowan, aspen, fuchsia, bracken and dog rose, and over all clambers a pretty flowering honeysuckle. From here you have a good view through the Rackwick Valley, which you traversed in Walk 27.

Follow the next arrow left, to cross the small burn. Look upstream to see a tiny waterfall, its crystal clear water hurrying through shadowing vegetation. The next sign directs you right, off the track and onto a narrow peaty path, as you begin to ascend the slopes of Moor Fea. Pass through the kissing-gate and stride on up through the heather, bog asphodel, bog cotton and tormentil.

As the path curves round a sheltered hollow, there is more soil, and bracken clothes the slopes, filling the air with its aroma. Enjoy the lovely view of Rackwick Bay. Another signpost appears beside the well made path, reassuring you that you are on the right route. Now you can see the rose-red cliffs of Rora Head, where fulmars fly in to their young.

Old Man of Hoy

Head on along the path, lined with deer grass in abundance. And then you have your first glimpse of the Old Man, the 450-foot high sandstone stack, perhaps Orkney's most famous landmark. Where the path descends through a rocky area, look for alpine bearberry, cowberry and crowberry — the latter in fruit — all growing beside the path.

Carry on along the flat path past, on the left, the little Loch of Stourdale. To the right large boulders litter the steep moorland slopes, and young great skuas perch on heather-covered mounds. Adults circle overhead and dive intimidatingly low when you come too close.

As the path leads towards the cliff edge, look for lousewort, bog asphodel, marsh orchis, scabious, tormentil and icelandic moss. The wind increases as you near the edge of the immensely steep cliffs, so take care as you approach. Then you can see the magnificent pink-red stack in all its dramatic entirety. A third of the way up, a couple of climbers appear like spiders. The first successful climb of the Old Man was in July 1966, by a team of three led by Chris Bonnington. It took them three days.

Return by the same route. You have a pleasing vista ahead all the way. Before you leave, you might like to visit the folk history display housed in a delightfully restored longhouse with flagged roof.

Here you can read about the 19th and early 20th century in Rackwick. It was a small but efficient fishing and crofting community. Although the land was reasonably sheltered and had a southerly aspect, fishing was extremely difficult.

The men went fishing from March to October. No boats could be anchored in the storm-tossed bay. Every spring the boat noust had to be cleared of large boulders before the fishing yawls could set sail. When they returned, the women waded out waist-deep in the water to haul them ashore. Then they carried home the catch on their backs. The boats required a crew of four and the fishing ceased in 1963 when not enough able-bodied men were left.

The original crofts were tiny, with a holding of one or two acres, but more land was reclaimed from the heather and the holdings were gradually enlarged. Most of the crofts had a milking cow and a few sheep, which were kept at home in the winter but taken to the heather in the summer. The children often acted as herders. The folk of Rackwick were skilled at rescuing sheep or seeking seabird eggs. Within the stone walls around the holdings the crofters had kale yards for growing cabbages, hay, oats and bere on the reclaimed land.

29. A Circular Walk from Betty Corrigall's Grave to Scad Head via Lyrawa Hill

Information	
Distance:	2 miles
Time:	1 hour
Map:	Landranger 7, Pathfinder 33 Stromness and the Old Man of Hoy, 36 Hoy (South), reference ND 281998 (parking grave)
Terrain:	Rough tracks, boots advisable.
Status of access:	Path by tolerance of landowner

Take the ferry to Lyness as for Walk 28 and drive north on the B9047. Park near Water of Hoy in the lay-by for Betty Corrigall's grave and walk down the peat track to the fenced, lonely grave. Betty was a young girl who lived in Lyness during the last century. She was in love with a sailor, but he left Hoy on a ship and never returned. Upon realising she was pregnant by him, she was so ashamed she tried to drown herself. Neighbours pulled her out and then she hanged herself in the byre. At the time suicide was considered a sin so she could not be buried in consecrated ground. The lairds of Hoy and Melsetter refused her burial on their estates and as a result she was buried on the parish border.

The grave was rediscovered in the early 1930s by peat cutters. In 1949 an American minister, the Reverend Kenwood Bryant,

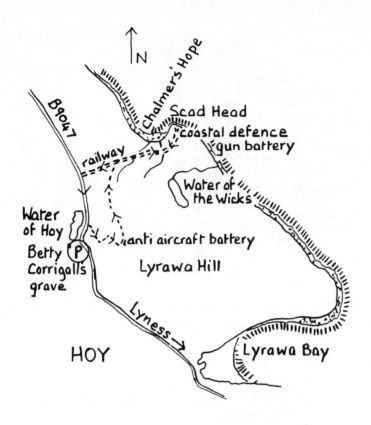

on a visit to Hoy, made a wooden cross and surrounded the grave with a picket fence. He asked Harry Berry, the Customs and Excise officer for Hoy, if he would make a gravestone and Mr Berry promised to do so when he had time. In 1976 he retired and found time to make the headstone. He wrote to Mr Bryant in the USA telling him he would now keep his promise. The minister replied that 'some people cannot keep a promise after 27 minutes let alone 27 years'.

The land around the grave is a peat bog and a heavy stone would require a deep foundation. Betty's grave had been disturbed twice in previous years so Mr Berry decided to make the headstone from fibreglass to avoid disturbing the grave again. As it was not known whether there had been a burial service, Mr Berry and two friends stood around the grave

Betty Corrigall's grave

one evening in 1976 and performed a short service. On a plaque in the lay-by is the following poem:

> So sweet
> So small
> Here lies Betty Corrigall
> Outwith the bounds of kin they buried her
> And not within
> The burn beside
> The brae above
> Keep her with more abundant love.

Today on the nearby lochan, the Water of Hoy, red-throated divers swim with their young and downhill from the grave a small plantation thrives and the lonely site seems less sad.

Walk up the narrow road (north) to take the red kissing-gate on the right. Beyond, follow the good track to the viewpoint of Lyrawa Hill, from where there is a wonderful panorama of Scapa Flow and Mainland. The indicator panel has lost its plate. From the plinth, walk left (north) to the derelict dugouts of a Second World War anti-aircraft battery. Between the buildings, look for a small slab of shale with a white arrow on it. This directs you down the slope, keeping above the bracken.

Carry on downhill, as directed by more of the arrowed slabs, until you reach a large metal wheel, once part of winding gear, and a sharply sloping track dipping towards the headland. Turn right and follow the route of what was once a railway track used for a coastal defence gun battery on the shore of the bay of Chalmers' Hope. Just before the derelict look-out buildings by the gun site, continue on a narrow green track that leads to Scad Head and more look-outs. What a view the soldiers had.

Black-backed gulls stand on the concrete roofs and sheep make use of the welcome shelter against rain, cold and heat. Rabbits scuttle over the rusted track of the rotating gun and traces of the old railway line. Seals peer from the water of the now peaceful bay. Wheatears, meadow pipits and stonechats flit about the heather, much as they must have done when the gun was ready for action.

Return along the green path to rejoin the bed of the old railway, which stretches upwards still, after 50 years, a great scar that can be seen from the ferry as you return. Continue past the winding wheel seen earlier and climb on to the road. Turn left to rejoin your car.

Instructions for the ferry — see Walk 28.

Meadow pipits

30. A Circular Walk on North Ronaldsay

Information	
Distance:	9 miles
Time:	7-8 hours
Map:	Landranger 5, Pathfinder 22 North Ronaldsay
Terrain:	Generally easy walking, except for part of the beach.
Ferry:	Telephone 01856 872044
Loganair:	Telephone 01856 872494
Status of access:	Path by tolerance of landowner

One boat a week serves the island of North Ronaldsay, weather permitting; it docks at the pier for a very short while. Times vary. Loganair does a very good daily (except Sundays) cheap flight, which gives you about eight hours on the island. The nine-seater plane, nicknamed the Flying Landrover, lands in a field used by cattle, so be prepared for manure splashing onto the windows as you land.

North Ronaldsay, with a population of 92 (36 households), is the most remote of the northern isles. Its narrow roads, almost traffic-free, are a joy to walk. Turn right out of the airfield and walk to the war memorial, where you turn right again. Stride along the road. Oyster-catchers alone disturb the peace on this quiet island with its unhurried pace of life. As you walk you feel that you have stepped back a few decades.

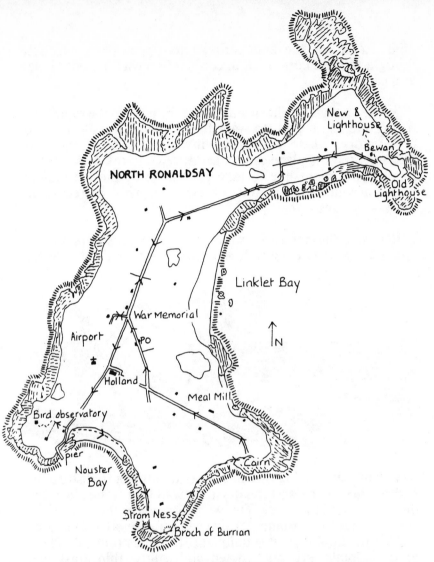

Continue past the stately Holland House on your left, owned by a descendant of the family who bought North Ronaldsay in the 18th century. Standing in front of the house are three cannon salvaged from a ship, *Crown Prince,* which was wrecked in 1744.

On the right is an attractive church built in the early 1800s. Beyond, in a field of cut hay, is a standing stone over 13 feet high. Look for the hole through its upper part, which is thought to have been used, in conjunction with a stone circle, as a calendar.

Stride on towards the pier and take the lane on the right, just before the cattle grid, to walk to the North Ronaldsay bird observatory, where visitors are made welcome. If the mist descends and the plane cannot get through to take you off the island, you might like to take advantage of the reasonably priced accommodation and perhaps help with the recording of observations.

Return to the cattle grid, which you do not cross, but instead pass through a gate opposite onto the silvery sands of Nouster

North Ronaldsay sheep

Bay. Walk left, taking care in June and July not to disturb the fulmars nesting against the drystone wall that stands between the pasture and the shore. This wall is known as the sheep dyke and is unique to the island. It runs right round North Ronaldsay and keeps the sheep (also unique) off the pastureland. These hardy animals feed on seaweed and a little thin grass that occasionally grows outside the walls. Close to lambing time the ewes are allowed onto pastures inside the walls for a few weeks.

Walk over the sand, where the sheep and ringed plovers leave their footprints, to Strom Ness point. Continue to a gate in the sheep dyke. This is the only means of access to the Brock of Burrian, part of an extensive Iron Age settlement. What a marvellous look-out site it provided.

Walk on along the rough shore — if in July and August, as quietly as you can — close to the sheep dyke, to avoid disturbing the seal colony with its many young. Overhead angry arctic terns mob, protective of their young. The birds nest in a marshy area where the water is almost completely colonised by flags.

Look for the gate leading from the beach, just beyond the fishermen's tall cairn topped with an old bell. Pass through the gate and walk the walled track, each stone of which is covered with lichen. The verge is ablaze with golden buttercups and yellow flags. To the right stands part of an old turf and stone dyke, called Muckle Gersty. It is one of two that divided the island into three and both could be pre-Norse. Legend has it that they were erected by three brothers who used them to apportion the island.

Stroll on to pass, on the right, a disused meal mill with two old millstones against the wall. Continue along the lane where, in a hay pasture, curlews, green plover, oyster-catchers and starlings feed together. At the cross-roads you have to make a decision. If you have spent too much time on the sands, then walk ahead to return to the airfield. But if you have a couple of hours to spare, turn right to pass the post office and village shop. Opposite is a building that houses fire-fighting equipment.

At the next road junction, bear right and stride the long narrow road which, after two miles, brings you to a sharp bend. Ahead, across Bewan Loch, stands the Old Lighthouse, built in 1789. It was unsatisfactory and the light was taken to Start Point on Sanday. The light was replaced by the ball of masonry you can still see.

Continue round the sharp bend to the New Lighthouse, first lit in 1853. It is 109 feet high, the tallest land-based lighthouse in the British Isles. It was automated in 1997.

Old Lighthouse

Notice as you walk the square walled enclosures known as punds used for dipping and clipping sheep. Look too for the circular enclosures, called plantiecrues in which seeds were planted, most likely kale. When the plants were strong enough they were planted out. Each croft had its own enclosure.

Return by the same route to the airport. If time is short someone will offer you a lift. No one in a vehicle seems to ignore anyone on foot — one of the pleasantries that make North Ronaldsay special.

31. A Short Walk through the RSPB Trumland Reserve

Information

Distance:	2 miles
Time:	1 hour
Map:	Use the RSPB's illustrated guide to the reserve. Landranger 6, Pathfinder 29 Wyre and Gairsay
Terrain:	Parts are rough and wet. Stout shoes, boots or wellingtons advisable.
Ferry:	Telephone 01856 751360 for ferry bookings (vehicles)
Status of access:	Path over RSPB land

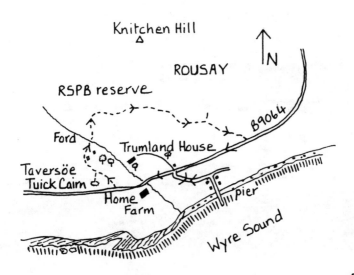

The island of Rousay lies across the Eynhallow Sound from Mainland. It is a hilly island with much heather moorland, and arable farming takes place around the fertile coastline. A road runs all round the island. It is narrow in parts, with passing places. In summer fuchsias bloom in profusion and the shoreline and much of the roadside are a mass of wild flowers. It has a great variety of bird life and a remarkably rich archaeological heritage.

The roll-on roll-off ferry, the *Eynhallow,* leaves from Tingwall on the north-east coast of Mainland. For this walk and Walk 32 a car is not needed because the reserve lies close to the pier. The journey across Eynhallow Sound and Wyre Sound takes 20 minutes and there are five or six crossings a day. The pier head at Rousay has excellent facilities, built in 1992.

Walk up the road from the terminal and at the T-junction, turn left. A neat well-cut hedge of fuchsia borders the way. Continue past Trumland House on the right, a Jacobean-style mansion, built for General Sir Frederick Traill Burroughs. His uncle, George William Traill, evicted 210 people during the Clearances in the mid-19th century — the only people in Orkney to suffer such a fate.

Trumland House

Opposite the stately house is Trumland Home Farm. Continue along the road to pass the woodland of the big house. Here grow many sycamores, laburnum, alder, willow, wych elm, ash and great masses of fuchsia. Climb steadily to a kissing-gate on the right. Pass through for the start of the trail and the entrance to Taversöe Tuick Cairn.

Alder tree

You see the cairn to your left. To gain access, walk past it to a gate at the top of the enclosure. Under the cairn's turf roof a concrete dome has a glass window, which allows plenty of light for viewing the well preserved site. The cairn is two-storeyed and a mesh gate gives access to the top level. The upper chamber is divided into two and has a recess in one of its walls. A metal ladder enables you to view the lower chamber, which was originally entered by a long passage at a lower level. It is divided into four compartments. Here skeletal remains, including a crouched skeleton, were discovered, resting on shelves. Lower still is a small chamber protected by a heavy trapdoor.

Much of the excavation work on this and other sites on Rousay, during the 1930s, resulted from the efforts of Walter Grant, the whisky magnate, who lived at Trumland House.

Return to the track from the gate and continue uphill to another kissing-gate beside a white-topped post. This post is the first of many and directs you through the reserve. Beyond the gate lies an old quarry. Head on to cross a narrow ford and continue over a dampish area to an old dyke and a ditch. Look for forget-me-nots, spearwort, broad-leaved pondweed, foxgloves and milkmaids.

Beyond the fence, follow the posts right to pass a large bank of fuchsia and meadow sweet. Now climb steadily through heather among which grows white bedstraw and male fern. As you climb the views become more extensive.

At the marker post carrying only the letters 'gt' on it (the remaining letters of 'long trail'), turn right. Walk the peaty track, following the posts, from where you can see the island of Wyre and the tip of Egilsay. Look for Wideford Hill (Walk 7) and Kirkwall on Mainland.

Great tracts of heather and crowberry, spangled with tormentil, stretch upwards to the top of the ridge. Rabbits squat quite still on the small patches of grass among the heather. Grouse droppings litter the way, but of the birds there is no other sign.

Follow the track, which is now edged occasionally with lousewort, as it swings right and then left. Below, you can see both Rousay pier and that on Wyre. At the telegraph pole this short walk is joined by the path that is part of the RSPB's longer trail (Walk 32).

The path descends steadily through more heather and then bushes of furze and fuchsia. Continue to a white marker post where the heather ceases and the arable land begins. Cross a small plank bridge, turn left, climb the stile and walk along the edge of the pasture. Look among the mass of daisies for dozens of mauve field pansies. Over the fence on your left grow vast numbers of fuchsia where you can see a pair of blackbirds and several young stonechats.

Climb the stile to the narrow road and turn right. What a contrast the flowers of the verge provide. Here grow in great abundance buttercups, hawkweed, yellow vetch and sow thistle. Cocks-foot grass now has ripe seed heads and plantain too. Hoodie crows and pigeons feed in the pasture.

Turn left at the signpost to return to the pier. On your way, look right into the last field before the houses, where grows a crop of bere barley, a tall plant bending its delicate head. Bere is grown only on Rousay where it is sometimes called corn (see Walk 3).

The RSPB have waymarked two walks — one of 2 miles and the other 4 miles. The reserve is always open. The warden's cottage is marked on the leaflet.

32. A Longer Walk in the RSPB's Trumland Reserve

Information

Distance:	4 miles
Time:	3-4 hours
Map:	The reserve provides a small informative leaflet. Landranger 6, Pathfinder 29 Wyre and Gairsay
Terrain:	This is a tough walk, often pathless and wet. Parts of it are over heather and through peat hags. Walking boots essential.
Status of access:	Path over RSPB land

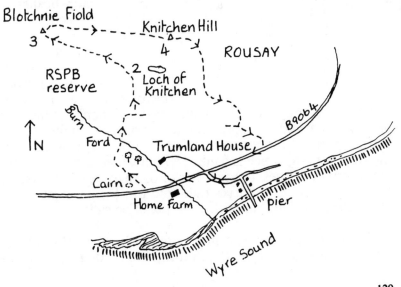

Reach the island of Rousay as for Walk 31. From the pier, walk the road to pass the excellent new waiting room. Turn left at the T-junction and head towards Trumland House and the home farm. The walk through the reserve starts at the signposted entrance to Taversöe Tuick Cairn (Walk 31). Stride the track up the slope, where fuchsias and low sycamores of Trumland House grow to your right. Look for ladder fern growing between the cams of the wall. Pass through the kissing-gate with the white-topped marker post beside it. (These marker posts are well placed and guide you safely over the high moorland.)

Continue past an old quarry and walk on to ford a small burn on convenient stones. Carry on over wet ground to a dyke and a ditch (white-topped post marked 1), which divide the moorland from the arable land. Look for forget-me-nots, milkmaids, spearwort, yellow flags and broad-leaved pondweed. Further along is a large bank of foxgloves.

Broad-leaved pondweed

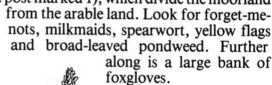

Climb the stile and follow the posts, which direct you past more bushes of fuchsia and m e a d o w sweet. Here a wren sings and a stonechat scolds from the top of a heather clump. Climb the steadily ascending path, lined with banks of heather on either side, and white bedstraw and tormentil. At the broken marker post with the letters 'gt' on it, turn left. Continue up the narrow path, which is banked with heather and crowberry. Hard fern flourishes in the shelter of these more hardy plants. Follow the path as it curves right and up. Meadow pipits flit about the moorland, uttering their plaintive calls.

Enjoy the views as you climb. Look for Kirkwall, the hills of Hoy and the end of Wyre. Bog cotton grows in damp patches as you come to the next marker post, which has an arrow directing you left. Here the path is indistinct so find the driest way to the next post (marked 2), which still directs you left. From here, look back to see Loch of Knitchen, where a red-throated diver floats buoyantly, resting with its head on its back. The RSPB asks you not to approach closer than the marker post, as the divers are easily disturbed.

The sunny bank by the path is bordered with primrose and violet leaves, as well as the pretty heath speedwell. Yellow bedstraw and dark blue milkwort also colour the way. Continue along what was a peat track. To the right fulmars nest on ledges in the exposed rock face. Cross the peat cuttings, following the posts, and keep climbing steadily. Look for the Old Man of Hoy away to your left. The track goes on and on and up and up. Away to the right you can see another marker post, but that indicates the route along the ridge and should be ignored.

Icelandic moss, bog asphodel and sphagnum moss grow about the peaty pools, and you will need to pick the driest route. Stride on until you reach post 3 and Blotchnie Fiold, where an amazing view waits. Look for Westray, Eday, Sanday, and North Ronaldsay on the northern horizon. To the south-west you can see Mainland and Hoy beyond. Below you can glimpse Peerie and Muckle Water, two inland trout lochs (see Walk 34).

Bog asphodel

This high point is the place for your picnic. Watch an arctic skua being harried by several angry oyster-catchers and great black-backed gulls gliding on barely flapping wings. Curlews fly across the slopes below.

Walk east along the ridge, following a line of marker posts that direct you towards a prominent cairn and a trig point on Knitchen Hill (4). Pause here for another tremendous view of almost all the islands of Orkney. See if you can spot the lighthouse on North Ronaldsay (Walk 30) and Foula and the Fair Isles. Here, watch and listen for golden plover, and for the trilling of skylarks. Here too a kestrel hunts for prey.

Drop down from the cairn to follow the ever-helpful posts over acres of heather. A female hen-harrier quarters the ground with easy flight. The posts direct you down another peat track, where grouse droppings litter the way.

Where the track swings left, below a telegraph post, the shorter RSPB reserve walk (Walk 31) joins it from the right. Press on past gorse and fuchsia to a marker post at the dyke between the moorland and the arable land. Cross a plank bridge, turn left and climb the stile. Walk across the pasture where field pansies grow. To your left is a mass of fuchsia and here a blackbird nests and a stonechat calls from the top of a bush.

Climb the stile to the road and turn right. Continue along the flower-bedecked way to turn left at the signpost for the pier.

33. The Westness Heritage Walk on Rousay

<table>
<tr><td colspan="2">Information</td></tr>
<tr><td>Distance:</td><td>2 miles</td></tr>
<tr><td>Time:</td><td>2 hours</td></tr>
<tr><td>Map:</td><td>Leaflet produced by the Department of Museums and Planning, Orkney Islands Council, who set up the walk. Land-ranger 6, Pathfinder 28 Dounby and 26 Rousay (North), reference HY 375307 (parking)</td></tr>
<tr><td>Terrain:</td><td>Level walking, but strong shoes required for path along shore.</td></tr>
<tr><td>Ferry:</td><td>The roll-on roll-off ferry leaves from Tingwall on Mainland — Telephone 01856 751360 for enquiries</td></tr>
<tr><td>Status of access:</td><td>Path created by agreement</td></tr>
</table>

Leave by the pier road and turn left at the T-junction. Drive for four-and-a-half miles and park in a well-signposted lay-by. Follow the signpost for Midhowe Cairn and Midhowe Broch and pass through a kissing-gate. Drop down the steepish slope to a black and white post and continue through another kissing-gate, walking in the same direction to the next post. Beyond lies Eynhallow Sound, with its fierce tide race.

Follow the wall on your right, with hay in the pasture to your left. Pass through the next signposted pasture to a kissing-gate.

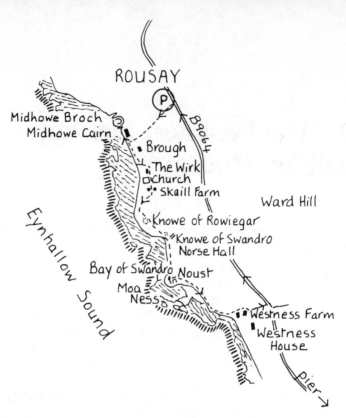

Walk right along the shore to a huge, sturdily constructed shed that shields a neolithic cairn, built around 3500 BC, from the elements.

Once inside, walk round the stalled, chambered cairn, the longest in Orkney, and then climb to the slatted platforms above for an exciting view. Look down to where the remains of 25 people were found lying facing inwards on the benches and chambers, and on the floor, in compartments formed by upright slabs. Animal bones were also found, showing that the people were both hunters and gatherers. Such tombs as these were used for many generations.

Leave this splendidly constructed building and continue along the shore to move forward three to four millenia in time to see Midhowe Broch. This fine defensive structure, which could house a small community, stands on the rocky shore.

Midhowe Broch

Geos, or creeks, on either side, effectively form a small and easily defensible promontory. On the landward side a strong wall stands between two ditches. Inside the broch there is a confusing mass of slabs, cells and part-walls but you can see that there was once an upper floor. Look for the glassed-over hearth and for the stone-slabbed water trough with a neatly fitting lid, into which water seeped, providing for the broch. The water still seeps in today.

Return along the shore and pass the cairn. Walk through the thrifts to come to the ruin of Brough Farm, which has gable ends and a cupboard remaining. It was built in the 18th century.

Walk on along the way and through a kissing-gate. Then turn right to pass behind The Wirk. Little remains today of what was once a 13th- or 14th-century ceremonial hall. The hall was at first-floor level and below was a basement of which you can just discern some parts.

Take the stile almost immediately on your right into the churchyard of the ruined former church of Rousay. It was probably built in the 16th or 17th century and was abandoned for worship in 1820, but burials continued until 1920. Look for two great buttresses erected to try to stop the church sliding into the sea.

Return out of the churchyard and stroll on to the next kissing-gate to walk through the ruined Skaill Farm. This was probably built at the same time as Brough Farm, seen earlier, and has been empty since the tenants were evicted at the time of the Clearances. Look for the kiln at the end of the barn, where barley was dried.

From now on the walk continues through the flower-covered turf just above the shore, where oyster-catchers, arctic terns, curlews, eiders, fulmars, great skuas, shelduck and shags can

Seals

all be seen. Seals lie off-shore. As you walk, you pass the Knowe of Rowieger, a chambered tomb, and the Knowe of Swandro, a mound which contains the remains of a broch. There is little to be seen — but imagination can do wonderful things.

Near the Knowe of Swandro, once stood two parallel long houses belonging to the Norse period of the 11th or 12th century. Carry on along the edge of the shore around Moa Ness promontory where, in 1963, a farmer digging a hole to bury a cow came across Pictish and Viking graves. Here an ornamental ringed pin, now known as the Westness Brooch, was found.

Further east, beyond the next marker post, stood a Viking noust. The Vikings could moor their boats nearby, even at low tide, and find shelter from wind and the strong tidal currents. On the inland side of the path stands a wet area fringed with flags. Here a pair of heron hunt for eels. As they fly off to their young on Mainland they are harried by angry oyster-catchers.

Cross over the bridge and continue to the kissing-gate just before Westness Farm and, beyond, walk beside the wall on your right, from where wheateaters call and where pied wagtails preen. Pass through the next kissing-gate to walk the farm access track. Turn left beyond the red-stained gate to walk to the road. To your right, almost obscured by sycamores, stands Westness House, once the home of General Traill Burroughs.

At the road, turn left and walk the quiet way, with glorious views of the Westness Walk and the Sound below, to rejoin your car.

The times and frequency of the Rousay ferry make it possible to walk to Westness and back. With transport you can fit in two walks and see more of the island.

34. A Short Walk to Inland Lochs above Westness House

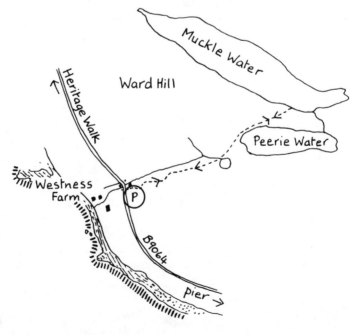

Park in the area close to the cottages, opposite the access to Westness Farm (three-quarters of a mile before the lay-by used in Walk 33). Take the track that climbs up into the hills to the right (south-east) of the cottages. Pass through the gate and continue, with Ward Hill standing dark and sombre to your left. Between the track and the hill lies a steep ravine through which hurries a tiny burn, edged with yellow flags. As you ascend, the ravine becomes narrower and more steep-sided.

Butterwort

Overhead fly oyster-catchers, curlews, greater black-backed gulls, fulmars and an arctic skua. The track climbs steadily, with a wealth of flowers growing along its margins. Look for tormentil, bed-straw, lousewort and marsh lousewort, butterwort, hard fern, crowberry, heather, heath speedwell, eyebright and primrose. Then you reach a small round dammed pool with reeds fringing its edges.

Continue walking to pass Peerie Water on whose banks grow two large clumps of salmonberry. Out in the middle of the still water idles a red-throated diver.

Willow

The track continues to the shore of the extensive Muckle Water. Here a low willow grows over its boulder-strewn margin. Return by the same route.

You may wish to combine this contrasting walk with the Westness Walk (Walk 33). As the track is on the land of James Marwick, the farmer at Westness Farm, please ask for permission to use it, which he gives readily. Shut the gate encountered first, keep all dogs on leads and do not approach vulnerable nesting birds.

35. A Circular Walk from Cross Kirk via Backaskaill Bay

Information

Distance: 3½ miles
Time: 2 hours
Map: Landranger 5, Pathfinder 27 Sanday Sound, 25
                Sanday (North), reference HY 653392 (parking)
Terrain: Easy walking all the way. Half the way is
                on quiet roads.
Ferry: Telephone 01856 872044
Status of access: Right of way

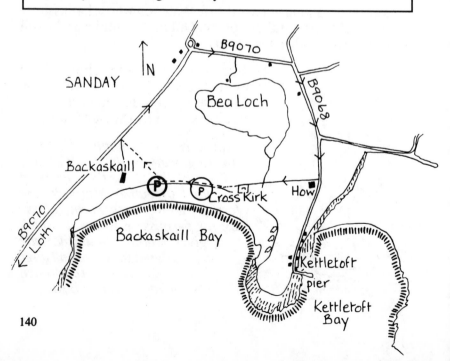

Travel by ferry to reach this lovely island of long sandy beaches and great tranquillity. The Orkney Islands Shipping Company's boat leaves Kirkwall pier and takes about two hours to reach the new deep-water pier at Loth.

From the ferry you can see Shapinsay with its grand Balfour Castle, much of Mainland, Rousay with its high hills, Hoy with its even higher hills often in mist, and Wyre and Egilsay, both green and low-lying. The ferry may call at Eday. Stronsay lies just across the sound. Then Sanday comes into sight.

Sanday Pier

Loth lies on the rather remote south-west coast of the island. Drive nine miles along the B9070, then turn right along the B9068 to Kettletoft, a picturesque village and harbour where the ferry used to call. It is well worth a visit.

From Kettletoft, return along the road to take a reinforced track that leads off left beyond the last building of How Farm on the edge of the village. Continue along the track, past the ruined Cross Kirk, to park on the left. The ruins date from the 16th century. It is believed that they stand on the site of a Viking settlement. Look for the extensive patches of pink and mauve eyebright and the delicate heartease surrounding the gravestones.

Leave this quiet corner. Turn left out of the gate of the grave-yard and head on along the track, which is edged with many colourful flowers. Continue beyond the barrier, following a narrow sandy path through the marram grass stabilising the dunes, to a wide steepish track leading to the white sands of Backaskaill Bay. Turn right and dawdle along the glorious shore, where seals laze in the sun and others peer curiously from the turquoise-blue sea. Pale mauve sea rocket grows in profusion. Overhead arctic terns screech and scold. Oyster-catchers pipe from pastures beyond the dunes and ringed plover chase in and out of the gently lapping waves.

After walking nearly half a mile, look for the gap in the dunes on your right 200 yards before Backaskaill Farm. Climb the fenced way to the metal gate. Beyond, pass the picnic area and walk the steadily ascending track. To the right, across the pasture, lies Bea Loch; close to this placid sheet of water the terns nest. Here too breed eider, shoveller, snipe and redshank. To the left lies the farm. Pass through another metal gate and walk to the road which comes from the ferry where you turn right. As you stroll, look for the very large flagstones used for roofing cottages and outhouses, and enjoy the view of the loch below in its shallow grassy depression.

Follow the road as it bears right and continue to the T-junction, where you turn right. As you near How Farm, turn right to walk the track to rejoin your car just beyond the ruined church.

Cows

36. A Linear Walk to Quoyness Chambered Tomb

Information

Distance:	1 mile
Time:	½ hour
Map:	Landranger 5, Pathfinder 27 Sanday Sound, 25 Sanday (North), reference HY 677388 (parking)
Terrain:	Easy walking.
Status of access:	Path by tolerance of landowner

Follow the instructions at the start of Walk 35 for travelling to Sanday. After driving six miles, turn right onto the B9068 and then take the second left, the B9069, signposted Lady Village. A mile and a quarter on, turn right at the signpost for Quoyness Chambered Tomb, directing you along a narrow track beside the Little Sea. The way soon becomes an impacted sandy track as it swings right along the southern side of the Little Sea. Park by a stone cottage where the track becomes reinforced. This is the access track to Elsness Farm, and it runs north along the shore of the Little Sea.

From the parking area, walk the grassy track beside the beautiful Sty Wick Bay. The water over the sand is a glorious turquoise, shading to purple. Seals laze on rocks and butterflies flit from flower to flower. Terns scream overhead. A family of eiders keep close together and redshanks hurry across the sand. Look back to see the magnificent curve of the bay.

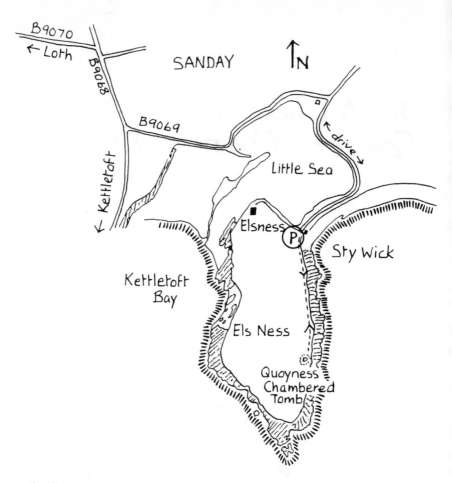

B9070

← Loth

B9068

SANDAY

↑N

B9069

← Kettletoft

drive →

Little Sea

Elsness

P

Sty Wick

Kettletoft Bay

Els Ness

Quoyness Chambered Tomb

Arctic terns

Continue until you reach the gate to the magnificent Quoyness Chambered Tomb. The entrance to the impressive rectangular chamber is low and narrow and requires you to crawl or crouch. A torch is provided. Once inside, admire the expert construction.

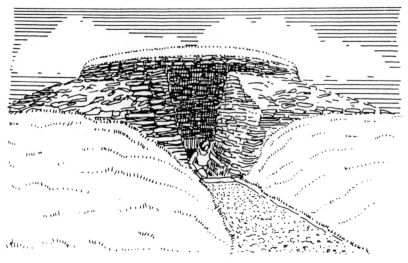

Quoyness Chambered Tomb

Small cells lead off the main chamber, each with a sturdy lintel. The cells are shaped like beehives. Again some crawling is required to see these.

This communal tomb dates from about 3000 BC, and is similar to Maeshowe on Mainland. Two carved stones and a bone pin resemble finds at Skara Brae. The remains of at least ten adults and four or five children were found in pits beneath the floor. Tombs such as this were used by many generations.

When you leave, you may continue round the Ness, keeping close to the shore, provided you obtain permission from Robert Seatter, the owner, at Elsness Farm, before you start the walk to the cairn.

37. A Circular Walk around Noup Head RSPB Reserve

Information

Distance:	2½ miles
Time:	2-3 hours
Map:	Landranger 5, Pathfinder 24 Westray, reference HY 402498 (parking)
Terrain:	Easy walking but beware dangerous cliffs.
Status of access:	Path over RSPB land

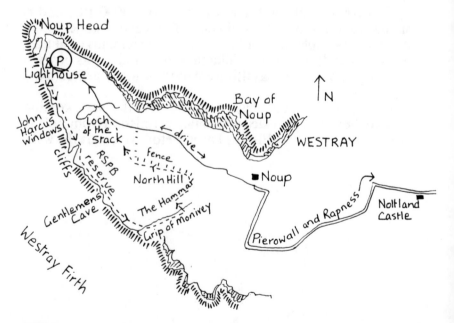

146

The roll-on roll-off ferry from Kirkwall usually berths at Rapness, not Pierowall as would appear on the Pathfinder map. There are few signposts on this delightful island, so you could have a confusing start to your visit if you drive off the ferry and set off believing you are at one landing place and are in fact at the other. . . .

To reach the Noup cliffs, drive along the B9066 to Pierowall, a large village on the edge of the Bay of Pierowall. Leave the village by a minor road west, in the direction of Noltland Castle. Beyond, drive on to pass Noup Farm and then take the continuing rough track to the lighthouse at the north of the RSPB reserve. The very white Noup Head lighthouse was constructed in 1898 and made automatic in 1964.

Park by the lighthouse wall. Walk south along the magnificent old red sandstone cliffs. The horizontal rock structure, composed of innumerable 'plates' of rock, provides unlimited sites for 50,000 nesting guillemots, 22,000 kittiwakes with young, and some razorbills and fulmars. The smell from the droppings of these birds in the breeding season can be overpowering.

Noup Head

The nearby waters provide a large amount of food for this huge number of birds.

Head south along the spectacular cliffs, with the sea to your right, over the short turf, which supports sea thrift and plantains. On your left watch for wheatears, great skuas, oyster-catchers, meadow pipits, redshanks and perhaps a Manx shearwater blown in by an earlier gale. Enjoy, with care, the dramatic views of the cliff faces, with layer after layer of rock stained white with bird excrement.

Kittiwakes

Stand on the trig point for an extensive view towards the island of Rousay. Continue on along the breath-takingly beautiful cliffs to pass two extremely deep geos. Then you can see a tall high cave far below. Next come John Harcus windows, where the cliff face, regularly fluted by the action of the sea, really does look like a row of windows.

As you walk, look for thyme, self heal, buttercups and hawkbit, all low-growing as a result of being cut back by the salt-laden winds. On the on-shore winds, attractively patterned young kittiwakes dive and zoom, as if imitating the antics of arctic terns. Far below, and just beyond the crashing white breakers, several shags fly, fast and low, over the surging swell.

Press on until just before you descend The Hammar. The Gentlemen's Cave lies in the sea cliffs far below. It can be reached from the cliff top, but you are advised not to attempt a descent without a local guide. Several Orkney lairds 'retired' to this cave after supporting the 1745 Jacobite Rebellion until their unfortunate allegiance was forgotten.

From below The Hammar, strike inland over turf spangled with grass of parnassus. Cross the little burn, Grip of Monivey, where lousewort flowers, and continue to the fence. Walk uphill with the fence to your right. Beyond it hoodies feed.

Ahead lies a delightful view of the Bay of Noup. Follow the fence all the way. Look for several hundred crab carapaces scattered over the turf, where countless greater black-backed gulls have feasted.

At the end of the fence strike across the turf, stepping across several narrow streams in the direction of the road and the lighthouse. Look for water crowfoot, growing in small pools. Continue past Loch of the Stack, where a pair of piratical arctic skuas, great masters of the air, create havoc among a large group of kittiwakes that are trying to idle the afternoon away on the still water.

Head on along the road to rejoin your car.

A new stiled path has been created from Noup Head to West Kirbist. Follow the clear green track along the cliffs to pass through some of the most dramatic cliff scenery in Orkney. Arrange for a taxi to meet you at West Kirbist after a three hour walk. Taxi: 01875 677450.

38. A Circular Walk from Noltland Castle

Information

Distance:	4 miles
Time:	2 hours
Map:	Landranger 5, Pathfinder 24 Westray, reference HY 429489 (parking)
Terrain:	Easy walking all the way.
Ferry:	See walk 37 for information on travelling to Westray.
Status of access:	Path by tolerance of landowner

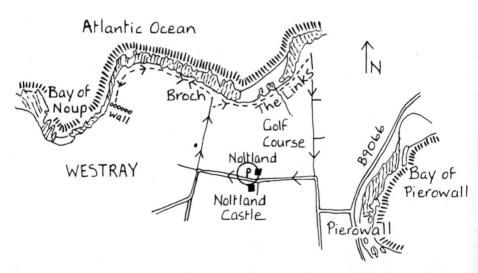

Park close to Noltland Castle, which lies on a minor road west of Pierowall. Do not obstruct the entrance to the farm — from where you obtain the key to visit. Noltland was erected in the second half of the 16th century by Gilbert Balfour. Legend has it that the castle is linked with the Gentlemen's Cave mentioned in Walk 37. It is a wonderful place to explore and must seem magical to all children. It is dramatic from the outside, with its many gun loops, but inside is even more so.

Leave the castle by the gate and turn left, west, to walk the narrow road until it turns sharp left. Here turn right and walk the reinforced cart track to its end. Pass through the metal gate on the right onto the links of Noltland. Look for the many walls of stone (dykes) for drying seaweed (tangle). The weed is collected in the autumn after gales have broken off the great strands and they have come ashore.

Carry on over the short turf, following the fence towards the magnificent sandy bay, where skerries turn the breakers white. Bear left to pass below a broch. Continue over the flower-covered turf, passing through two Orkney gates, and on to the drystone wall. This is the end of land belonging to William

Tangle dykes

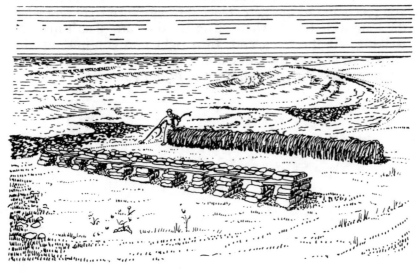

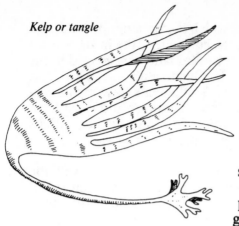

Kelp or tangle

Brown, the farmer who is keyholder for the castle and who has allowed the author to include this walk.

From the wall you have a splendid view of the route of Walk 37. Return back along the coast past shallow depressions where seaweed was burnt to produce kelp, once used in glass and soap making and for obtaining iodine. Further on are more tangle dykes.

Over the wire fencing on the right, among dunes, is an archaeological dig. Here in the late 1970s an extensive area of prehistoric settlement was excavated. The houses and middens were contemporary with Skara Brae (3000 BC). The excavation trenches have been covered over and work is suspended for the time being.

Beyond the dig lies the golf course. Carry on to step across a small burn and stroll on along the links above the shore until you reach an Orkney gate. Once through, turn right and walk the long wide track, where silver weed creates a soft mat for walking. At the track end, turn right and continue up the narrow road, past the golf clubhouse, surely the smallest ever. Carry on past the football pitch to rejoin your car.

39. A Circular Walk along the Bay of Cleat

Information

Distance:	3½ miles
Time:	2 hours
Map:	Landranger 5, Pathfinder 24 Westray, reference HY 462471 (parking)
Terrain:	Easy walking but long grass in parts could be wet. Stout shoes advisable.
Status of access:	Path by tolerance of landowner

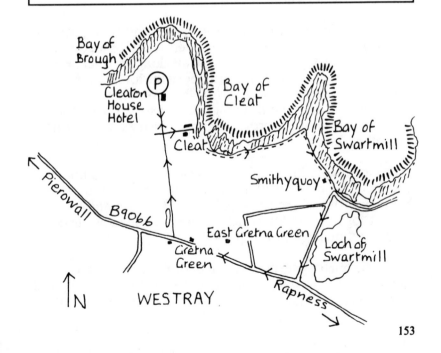

Cleaton House Hotel

Park in the car park at the back of Cleaton House Hotel. The owner welcomes walkers and makes a very good cup of tea. From the hotel walk up the access drive. Look over the wall on the right to see a flock of grey plover. These lively, noisy birds run quickly over the ground as they feed, constantly giving their shrill, penetrating call.

On either side of the hotel, cheviot sheep and cattle graze. At the cross of roads and tracks, turn left to stride a good cart-track. Walk through Cleat Farm and on along the track. Follow it as it bears right to continue just above the lovely shore, from where there are good views across to Papa Westray. Redshanks, ringed plovers and one or two greenshanks call from the bay as they busily hunt for prey. A family of eiders, whispering to each other, bob on the waves.

The sorrowful singing of the seals alerts you to their presence. In spite of their size, the animals are superbly camouflaged as they laze on the seaweed-covered rocks. Both grey and common consort together. Fulmars nest on the very shallow cliffs and adults continually fly in with food.

Pass through a gate that has a pair of fine stone pillars. Walk on the continuing way, which is now almost obscured by lush vegetation that makes walking harder. Eventually you have to leave the land for the shore, the track having been eroded by the sea. If during an exceptionally high tide this is not possible, then climb the fence and continue along the pasture.

Above the high tide line the shore is covered by dark green orache, with sea rocket, mayweed and silver weed growing among it. Press on past a dwelling named Smithyquoy. Join the metalled road, which runs by the shore, to walk inland beside the Loch of Swartmill. Here a heron rises and flies off over the bay.

On joining the main road, the B9066, turn right and continue along the almost traffic-free road. Carry on past the telephone box and then a house called East Gretna Green. The next dwelling is called Gretna Green. Beyond, you turn right to walk a grassy track. This passes a small pool on the left. Stroll on to the cross of tracks and continue to the hotel, which lies ahead.

Eider ducks

40. A Circular Walk via Westside Church

Information

Distance:	2½ miles
Time:	1-2 hours
Map:	Landranger 5, Pathfinder 24 Westray, reference HY 455437 (parking)
Terrain:	Easy walking all the way.
Status of access:	Path created by agreement

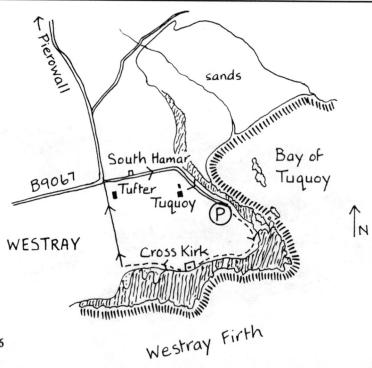

Drive south out of the village of Pierowall and take the B9067, which is signposted to Westside Church. At the next signpost for the church, turn left and drive to the end of the metalled track and on along the continuing track to a parking area on the shore of the Bay of Tuquoy.

Stroll on to pass through the red painted kissing-gate. Walk the fenced track that keeps close to the lovely shore. Continue round the Point o' the Scurroes to pass through the next kissing-gate. Beyond, walk across the pasture, which is covered with daisies and buttercups. Fulmars nest on the shallow cliffs and oyster-catchers pipe as they fly overhead.

Great plates of red sandstone project out into the water. From the shore ahead six herons fly up and circle above. Across Westray Firth you can see the high hills of Rousay.

Climb the ladder stile into the graveyard of Cross Kirk, now a ruin. This church, probably built by the Viking Haflidi of Tuquoy, was dedicated to the Holy Cross. The square-ended chancel, which was vaulted, and the east end of the nave, were built in the 12th century. The west end of the nave was a later

Cross Kirk

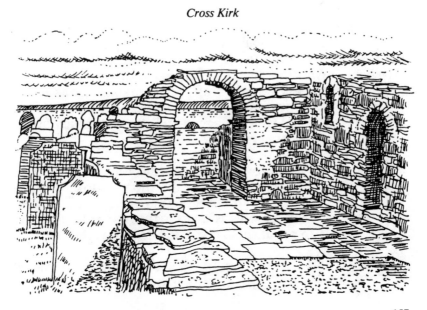

157

addition. The original entrance and the only surviving window are still preserved in the south wall of the nave.

Look at the dates on some of the headstones. A moving script gives the following details of deaths in one family:

> James died aged two
> William twenty-six
> Isabella fourteen
> Mary Ann twenty-five
> John fourteen
> Maggie twenty-five
> Jessie fourteen
> George killed in the First World War twenty-seven
> Thomas also died in the Great War
> Their father lived until he was seventy-four.

Leave the church by the gate and walk a few yards to pass under the wire fence, just above the shore. Here, in the low cliffs, can be seen the edge of a large Norse settlement. The sea is gradually eroding the cliffs but you can see some of the midden and stones of a dwelling. This area was extensively excavated 20 years ago.

Pass through the next kissing-gate and then follow the track right, to walk inland. Continue past the dwelling *Stonecrop* Tufter to the crossroads, where you turn right. Walk the quiet road (which you drove along earlier) to pass a ruined croft, South Hamar. Look for its kiln, now with grass and nettles growing out of the top. Its roof is flagged and supports much bright yellow stonecrop.

Stroll towards the sea and follow the track as it continues above the shore. Look for turn-stones, with bright orange legs, using their pick-axe bills as levers to throw over large stones to get at small crabs and sand-hoppers.

Continue along the flower-bordered way to rejoin your car.

41. A Circular Walk on North Hill RSPB Reserve

Information

Distance:	3½ miles
Time:	2-3 hours
Map:	Landranger 5, Pathfinder 23 Papa Westray.
Terrain:	Easy walking — there is no peat on Papa Westray.
RSBP Warden:	Telephone 018574 644240
Community Co-op:	Telephone 018574 644267
Loganair:	Telephone 01856 872494
Ferry:	Telephone 01856 872044 and 01857 677216
Status of access:	Path over RSPB land

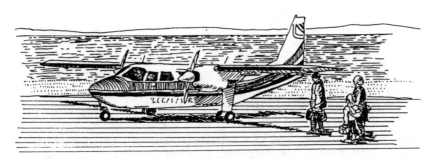

Flight to Papa Westray

Several ferries serve Papa Westray each day and there are two flights. Both means of transport should be experienced.

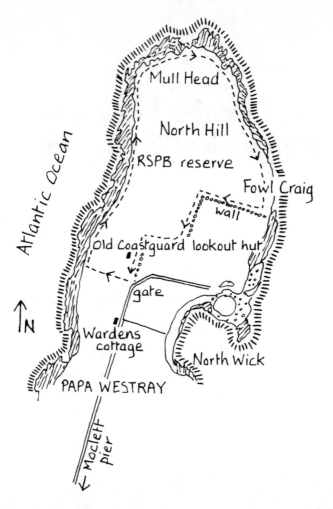

From Moclett pier it is three miles to the North Hill RSPB reserve. Book a taxi if you wish to spend most of your day bird watching. But islanders are very kind and welcoming and you will most likely be offered a lift over the three miles to the far end of the island. The one narrow road runs through fertile land, with the sea on either side. Just before the bird sanctuary, call in to the pink cottage (Rose Cottage) on the left, where the bird warden may be available to accompany you on your walk round the glorious cliffs of North Hill. Even if you wish to 'go it alone', he would like to know that you are on the island. Please remember visitors must **NOT** walk through the tern colony. The warden might be one of the people offering you a lift from the ferry.

An information board at the gate of the reserve requests that, if you are walking during the May, June or July breeding season, you should walk round the edge of the cliffs. This is sheer pleasure at any time.

North Hill is communally owned by the islanders and there is controlled grazing. The community and the RSPB together manage this wonderful site. From the gate, walk up the slope to the bird hide, which is situated in an old coastguard lookout hut, splendidly windproof. In the breeding season you can view Britain's largest nesting colony of arctic terns. Among this wonderful, noisy, screeching assembly nest many arctic skuas, who obtain their food from the terns by flying them down until they disgorge their catch. The colony has not always been so successful in maintaining numbers, which is why visitors should view but not approach.

From the hide, return to the gate and follow the fence for 50 yards to the western cliffs, and then walk north over the maritime sedge heath. Look for sea thrift, thyme, crowberry, bearberry, scabious, lousewort, butterbur, sea plantains, sedges, field gentians and large numbers of grass of parnassus. Continue on past shallow depressions where seaweed was burnt to produce kelp (see Walk 38). Now the hollows are colonised by low growing willow, making the most of the shelter.

To the west the huge Atlantic rollers pound the rugged sandstone shore. Large numbers of red-legged, squeaking black guillemots sit in small gossiping groups on ledges to the lee of

Gannets

wind. Gannets fly high over the waves and then make their spectacular dives after fish. Little dark birds fly low over the water, a little nearer to the shore than the gannets. These are puffins and razorbills, now enjoying freedom from parenting.

Large numbers of kittiwakes, many still in immature plumage, sail and glide overhead. On the great sheets of sandstone, which tilt into the breakers, rock pipits busily hunt insects, cheeping quietly as they do so. Continue past more tangle dykes (low walls) to walk over yellow bedstraw brightening the turf. Pass round Mull Head and continue along the cliffs, now heading south.

Walk over the top of Fowl Crag, a nesting site for large numbers of razorbills, kittiwakes and guillemots. Close views of the birds can be enjoyed from a wide platform of rock close by. The last great auk was shot here in 1813. It is now on display in the Natural History Museum in London.

On reaching a drystone wall, walk to the right of it and begin looking for the Scottish primrose. This rare diminutive plant, which is thought to have survived the Ice Age, grows in profusion. On each small plant, look for several tiny purple flowers, each with a yellow centre or 'eye'.

Continue to walk inland, keeping to the right of the stone walls to return to the entrance gate.

42. A Circular Walk via Knap of Howar and Holland

Information

Distance:	5 miles, plus 3 miles to the start
Time:	3-5 hours
Map:	Landranger 5, Pathfinder 23 Papa Westray
Terrain:	Easy walking but boots advisable.
Telephone Nos:	See Walk 41.
Status of access:	Path by tolerance of landowner

See Walk 41 for details of travel to Papa Westray. If you have one day only, it would be better to start the walk at the bird reserve (Walk 41). You may wish to walk the three miles to the gate, or to savour fully the five-mile return walk, obtain a lift, or order a taxi.

Pass through the bird reserve gate and follow the wall on your right. Continue beside other walls, until, just before you reach the east shore south of Fowl Crag, you see a gate on your right. Before you pass through you may like to look for Scottish primrose growing in profusion ten yards from the west side of the wall running north-south above the Crag.

Beyond the gate, turn left and walk to the shore, where huge breakers crash on the extensive flags of sandstone. Edge the small reedy Loch of Taing and continue along the attractive, curving shingle beach of North Wick. Here a vast expanse of silvery sand, with many shells, provides safe swimming. Just

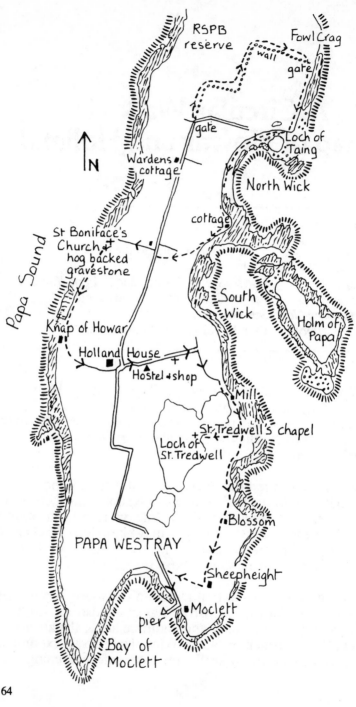

RSPB reserve

Fowl Crag

wall

gate

gate

Loch of Taing

Wardens cottage

North Wick

cottage

St Boniface's Church
hog backed gravestone

Papa Sound

South Wick

Holm of Papa

Knap of Howar

Holland House

Hostel & shop

Mill

St Tredwell's chapel

Loch of St. Tredwell

Blossom

PAPA WESTRAY

Sheepheight

Moclett

pier

Bay of Moclett

offshore a long skerry supports many seals, which sing quietly, and sometimes eerily to each other.

Eiders swim in shallow turquoise water and ringed plovers race in and out of the gentle waves. Across the bay you can see the Holm of Papa and its ancient cairns. (To visit the Holm of Papa, ask at the Co-op about a boat, allowing one hour on the holm.) In the low dunes fringing the bay grow lyme-grass, sea rocket and sea mayweed. Just at the headland, before you enter the next bay, South Wick, stands a stone cottage. The cottage has had to be rebuilt twice, each time further inland, because of intense erosion by the sea.

Stroll on along the lovely bay until you reach a sturdy stone cairn on the shore. Here, above the sand and its grassy margins, you join a track where two convenient seats enable you to eat your lunch while enjoying a marvellous view of the Holm of Papa. Head on along the track, which turns inland before a cottage. Follow the track as it swings left and then up the slope to the road. Here turn right and then, at the next cottage, left, to follow the sign for St Boniface's Church. Walk down the reinforced track, with a glorious view of Papa Sound ahead.

Enter the churchyard through the white kissing-gate to where fuchsia grows close beside the orange-lichened walls. To the east side a wooden cover shields a Norse hog-backed gravestone. Lift the cover. The gravestone is shaped like a longhouse and in the sunlight you can just make out patterning on what would have been the roof.

Norse hog-backed gravestone

Go into the church, which is being carefully restored, and enjoy its immense peace after the wind outside. Its walls date from the 12th century. The church stands on an area known as 'Monker Hoose', a huge Iron Age settlement. Leave by the gate and walk left beside the church wall, noting to your right a huge grass-covered mound that possibly dates from between the 11th to the 13th century.

Climb the stile over the fence and walk right (north) to reach the shore. Turn left and walk behind the church to see a sad archaeological site. Here the midden and stonework of a settlement that was occupied for more than a thousand years is being gradually eroded by the sea.

Carry on along the shore (south) over the great flags of sandstone. Beware of young fulmars, plump and downy, sitting on their ledge waiting to be fed. When disturbed they can, with some accuracy, eject a stream of a strong-smelling oily substance.

Head on to reach the Knap of Howar, a neolithic farmhouse cared for by Historic Scotland, who provide an information panel. It tells that the settlement was established about 3500 BC. It lay well back from the seashore in a grassy area separated by dunes from a broad sandy bay. Over the years the ruins were buried by sand, then revealed again. It is the oldest known building in Orkney. The farmers who lived there grew cereals and raised cattle and sheep. They ate shellfish gathered from the shore. They would have fished, hunted for game and caught wildfowl, very much as island people did until modern times. They had no metals and made all their tools from stone or animal products such as whalebone.

Fulmars

Leave the fascinating site and walk inland to pass through a large wooden gate to a walled track. This leads to Holland House and its many out-buildings. It was built in the 17th century by the Traills and passed out of the family in 1952. It is now owned by John and Annie Jean Rendall, who welcome visitors. Knock on the door to obtain an informative leaflet and wander at leisure around the farm. Do not miss the horse mill tramp, the machinery of which was driven by six horses; the dovecote, where pigeons were kept for the laird's use; the old barn where sheaves were laid on the floor and the grain knocked off with wooden flails; and the kiln, where grain was dried.

Leave Holland House and walk down the signposted road to pass the Community Co-op, which offers a youth hostel, guesthouse, self-catering cottage and well-stocked shop. Stroll on to pass the church and the school. Bear right at the T-junction to walk a cart-track. Take the arrowed stile beside the gate to continue just above the sandy bay.

To the right lies Loch of St Tredwell. Pass on the landward side of the old water mill, used about a hundred years ago for milling oats. You can see two millstones and the remains of what would have been an undershot wheel made necessary by the low level of the loch. Beyond, you step across the old leat which carried water from the loch to the wheel.

Head on along the shore, where a huge assembly of arctic terns and kittiwakes sun and preen. Follow a cart-track that swings right to a gate. Beyond, continue right to walk a fenced grassy track, which swings right again and brings you to the shore of the loch and the remains of St Tredwell's Chapel, built on an artificial peninsula. The chapel stands on top of the ruins of a broch. St Tredwell's was a medieval holy place and a pilgrimage centre. Eye diseases were supposed to be cured by water from the loch.

Return along the fenced track and on to come close to the shore. Climb the stone stile and pass tangle dykes to walk what soon becomes a good footpath. Go through the Orkney gate, continue between a wall and a fence, and then past a ruined farm, named Blossom. Beyond the next gate, keep close to the fence on your right. Bear slightly left to join the farm track at the next farm, Sheepheight. Follow the way right until you join the road to the pier, where you turn left.

Enjoy the glorious carpet of flowers, including a multitude of grass of parnassus, as you stroll to pick up the ferry.

You may wish to combine Walks 40 and 41.

Clan Walks

A series of walks described by Mary Welsh, covering some of the most popular holiday areas in the Scottish Highlands and Islands.

Titles published so far include:

1. 44 WALKS ON THE ISLE OF ARRAN
2. WALKS ON THE ISLE OF SKYE
3. WALKS IN WESTER ROSS
4. WALKS IN PERTHSHIRE
5. WALKS IN THE WESTERN ISLES
6. WALKS IN ORKNEY
7. WALKS ON SHETLAND
8. WALKS ON ISLAY
9. WALKS ON CANNA, RUM, EIGG & MULL
10. WALKS ON TIREE, COLL, COLONSAY AND A TASTE OF MULL

OTHER TITLES IN PREPARATION

Books in this series can be ordered through booksellers anywhere. In the event of difficulty write to Clan Books, The Cross, DOUNE, FK16 6BE, Scotland.